PLAYS ONE

Bryony Lavery's plays include *Last Easter*, *A Wedding Story*, *Her Aching Heart*, *Flight and Bag*; and adaptations of *Behind the Scenes at the Museum* and *The Magic Toyshop*. Her most celebrated work, *Frozen*, which opened first at Birmingham Rep, then at the Royal National Theatre in July 2002, staring Anita Dobson, Josie Lawrence and Tom Georgeson, was nominated for a Tony Award and won the TMA Best New Play Award and the Eileen Anderson Central Television Award for Best Play. She is an Honorary Doctor of Arts at De Montfort University. Future work includes Angela Carter's *Wise Children* for the Royal National Theatre, *The Thing With Feathers* for the McCarter Theatre, Princeton, USA and *Dirt* for Manhattan Theatre Club.

BRYONY LAVERY

Plays One

A Wedding Story

Frozen

Illyria

More Light

ff

faber and faber

First published in 2007
by Faber and Faber Limited
3 Queen Square, London WC1N 3AU

Typeset by Country Setting, Kingsdown, Kent CT14 8ES
Printed in England by Bookmarque, Croydon, Surrey

A CIP record for this book
is available from the British Library

ISBN 978-0-571-23465-3

2 4 6 8 10 9 7 5 3 1

Contents

Introduction

Here's the story of a bus journey I took once.

It was in India, going from Chandigar to Simla.

I was on my own in a strange, beautiful country.

That morning, I was having such a good conversation at the hotel, and such a splendid breakfast, I was nearly an hour late arriving at Chandigar bus station, but the bus *before* the one I had planned to catch was still sitting in its bay so I got on that.

I had much more luggage than I needed but I could not bear to ditch any of it.

With a lot of smiling, interested help, I loaded it all onto the back seat.

Crammed to the gills with far too many passengers and far too much *stuff*, the bus set off.

After a few miles, the bus driver stopped at a small roadside shrine and we all debused, prayed, ate *prasad* and had red holy dots put on our foreheads. Watched over by the gods, we biffed off again in our ancient, fragile vehicle, swaying and groaning over the tarmac bumps and holes.

We sometimes kept to our side of the road. Mostly, though, not.

We stopped for regular meals . . . second breakfast, elevenses, early lunch, lunch, late lunch, afternoon tea, *serious* afternoon tea, early supper, early evening snack . . .

We cleverly used the refreshment stops as toilet breaks to save time on our journey.

Characters got off, characters got on.

Small stories unravelled over the tired, hard seats.

Vendors at every stop provided us with a lot of bright things we did not really need.

Once, a small, brief, nasty punch-up occurred up at the front between two freeloading riders, the bus driver and the people sitting near the bus driver.

We at the back pretended not to see it.

On a particularly dashingly-taken bend, somebody's cook pot and lid fell out through the always-open door. We stopped, chased them down the road and into the undergrowth, caught them, put them safely back on the bus and tooled off again, the open door now wedged with my expensive camera case.

We were bored, interested, awake, asleep, alert, dull.

Three-quarters into our journey, when we were all a bit hot and quarrelsome, a large vital piece of our bus's engine fell off onto the road.

We all piled out.

Stood with our luggage and cook pots making polite conversation.

The bus I had *meant* to catch arrived.

We all clambered aboard our new vehicle.

The old bus, half in the forest, looked forlorn.

The new bus began to climb.

Up a curving, snaking road through the lush bright green forest.

Monkeys sitting in our path watched us scornfully.

Then, in their own good monkey time, got off their bright red bottoms and falolloped off into the undergrowth.

The road got steeper.

The bus got wheezier.

The air grew thinner, colder.

Until finally we arrived at the top of the mountain.

In the clear blue beautiful air of Simla.

*

Just a travel story?

No.

The nearest I can come to a metaphor for what it's like writing a play.

*

I'd like to thank all the directors, actors, designers, lighting designers, stage crew, audiences . . . well, *everyone* who took the perilous journeys on the buses bound for *Illyria*, *Frozen*, *A Wedding Story* and *More Light*. So many ideal travel companions.

Bryony Lavery, August 2006

A WEDDING STORY

Acknowledgements

Lines from *Casablanca* by kind permission of Warner Bros.

Sally Cline, *Lifting the Taboo: Women, Death and Dying*

Elisabeth Kubler-Ross, *The Wheel of Life*

Sherwin B.Nuland, *How We Die*

Death, Dying and Bereavement, ed. Donna L. Dickenson, Malcolm Johnson and Jeanne Samson Katz

A Wedding Story was first performed by Birmingham Repertory Theatre Company and Sphinx Theatre Company at The Door, Birmingham Repertory Theatre, on 2 November 2000. The cast was as follows:

Sally Jackie Clune
Peter Andrew Hawkins
Robin Brendan O'Hea
Grace Aicha Kossoko
Evelyn Kika Markham

Director Annie Castledine
Designer Ruari Murchison
Lighting Designer Nick Beadle
Composer Timothy Sutton
Movement Janette Smith

Characters

Evelyn
a married woman

Peter
a husband

Sally
a daughter

Grace
a woman in love

Robin
a son

Author's Note

This play is laid out to help the actors find
the true rhythms of dramatic speech.

None of the characters speak in sentences
or observe punctuation or breathe at the right time.

Because   often
They are in   torment.

The short lines, the spaces within or between lines,
are there on purpose to indicate the subtext and
to help the performer to find the physical
and emotional journey within a speech.

I hope the reader will observe the deliberate
eccentricities of my punctuation . . .

ONE
A GOOD LAUGH

We are in fog.

In it, a room of today hangs expectant.

Preparations for a small wedding. Clothes, shoes, hats, gifts. A water source.

Our characters appear and disappear in the partnership between light and fog.

The dramatic, introductory music to Casablanca *plays as we see . . .*

Evelyn watching television . . . Casablanca . . . very focused . . . as if studying it . . .

Casablanca
'With the coming of the Second World War
many eyes in imprisoned Europe
turned hopefully, or desperately,
t'ward the freedom of the Americas . . .
Lisbon became the great embarcation point . . .
but not everybody could get to Lisbon directly . . .
and so a tortuous roundabout refugee trail sprang up
Paris to Marseilles
across the Mediterranean to Oran
then by train, or auto, or foot
across the rim of Africa
to Casablanca in French Morocco
here the fortunate ones, through money
or influence, or luck
might obtain exit veez-ays
and scurry to Lisbon
and from Lisbon to the New World
but the others wait in Casablanca

and wait
and wait

and wait . . .

Throughout this, Evelyn . . .

Evelyn (*watches intently, then*)
Oh!

It is something she recognises . . .

ah!

She points an oldish finger at what she recognises . . .

ah!

There is something very interesting and nice there . . .
She smiles.

ha.

She watches intently, a smile on her face. Her eyes
move with her head as she watches different details in
all parts of the screen . . .

hmmm.

mmmm.

mmmmmmmm.

The smile broadens. She points again . . . this time
particularly . . . at some detail which makes her
laugh . . .

ha!   ha!

The detail continues to amuse her.
She laughs delightedly and delightfully for a long
time at what is going on on the screen.
She is completely amused and in absolute hilarity.

ha ha ha ha ha ha ha!

Tears roll down her cheeks and she wipes them away,
still laughing.

ha ha ha   (*Sniff.*)   hhaaaa haaaaa . . .
haahaahaaa . . . (*Wipe.*)

Somewhere near, someone arrives.

oh!

She has heard. It is very perturbing, unexpected. Her
face is completely anxious . . .
    Nearer this time . . . another sound only she hears,
approaching, until . . .
    Peter, semi-smartly dressed in a suit, the wrong
shoes, enters . . .

Evelyn (*with a joy equal to that for the video*)
Ah!

They kiss, embrace . . . this is the great romance . . .
as . . .

Peter
You should have come, darling!
You would have loved it!
I'm a little the worse for the drink . . .

He is quite drunk . . .

so much photographing and videoing
to get through we didn't sit down to the *Tuck*
until three so Bucks Fizz and then just Fizz
then just Bucks
and then the father of the girl who
married the *other* brother with the small
catering business who could have
banged out a *much* better three-course
deal if they'd come to *him* bought me a
Beer

and then we saw *Draught* Guinness and
Beer and . . .
But what a *magnificent* wedding!
Everybody asked after you . . .
I was a little late . . .
big pile-up on the M-something . . .
took a clever little detour . . .
then the bloody map didn't fit the roads! . . .
arrived just at the 'Do you, Michael,
take thee, Charlotte . . .' stage . . . Evelyn . . .
they were videoing the whole bangshoot
in the church!
What's it all coming to?
. . . I mean, is that allowed, ecclestiastically?
. . . ?
well, *must* be . . .
vicar moving into shot . . .
it's all a bit fly-on-the-pulpit for me but . . .
I oozed into a pew doorside of it all . . .
luckily the *correct* side . . . *our* side, darling . . .
so . . . a lot of 'vaguely marriage' clothes . . .
flung-together outfits . . .
lots of loose tickets in sort-of-smart
and 'oh-they'll-do' shoes.

Peter looks at his own 'they'll-do' shoes.

Evelyn

Tut tut tut! (*They won't do for her.*)

Peter

I know I know . . . but *this*

He demonstrates his bizarre outfit.

how-d'you-do was right at home!

*Evelyn picks confetti off his clothes . . . straightens . . .
as . . .*

Their side   spanking new
money had been *spent*
money was *no* object . . .
bridesmaids in peacock blue
pages . . . a sort of mini-Press Gang from
Nelson's bloody navy type of thing! I mean!
Groom and the men and whatnot
dressed as the the Ascot scene from
the *Pygmalion* film . . .

Snaps his fingers until:

. . . *My Fair Lady*!!
And . . .
I've never seen so many bridesmaids and
pages and
babies
wrapped up like lamb chops outside
a Royal Wedding . . .
a child hiccuped throughout . . .

Evelyn
   Ha.

Peter
   you know when you get hiccups . . .?

   Both really do know how she gets hiccups . . .

Peter
   Louder than you . . . church very good acoustics . . .
   it hiccuped right through the vows,
   several prayers
   and 'Love Divine'
   stopped only by the Vicar's Address . . .
   whose speciality is clearly . . . *jokes*!!
   Did . . . 'the bride looks at the church . . .
   she sees . . .

He acts this out.

the *aisle* . . .
the *altar* . . .
the *hymn* . . .

Peter
aisle
altar
hymn . . .

"*I'll alter him*!"
she thinks!'

Evelyn
'I'll alter him!'

She laughs delightedly. So does Peter . . . then . . .

Peter
Very pleased our daughter was behaving herself
at this . . .
just kept her head down . . .
looked . . . *quietly ironic* . . .!

Both Peter and Evelyn react similarly to this . . .

and then . . .
outside the church for *more* photo
opportunities . . .
I'm taking a photograph of the bride and bridesmaids
at the gate . . .
and I think . . . 'Hey, wait a minute . . .'
the bridesmaids were
in peacock blue and now they're in eau de nil . . .
and . . . I realise
I'm photographing the *next wedding*!

*Peter laughs out loud . . . spluttering . . . Evelyn
laughs delightedly too . . .*

Evelyn
> Ha ha ha ha ha!

Peter
> I apologise with unctuous charm . . . 'I'm sorry . . . but
> you all looked so *lovely* . . .' and then . . .
> it all got a bit . . . whatsisname . . . Philip Larkin . . .
> we're all following the antique black and white Rolls
>   Royce to
> the reception . . .
> and over the motorway . . .
> on one of those bridges . . .
> a horse and carriage with *another* bride . . .
> going *over* us . . .
> and as we're eating our salmon en croute, peas . . .
> *lemon* potatoes . . .
> indifferent Chablis . . .
> in The Coachman Suite . . .
> the eau de nil crew are on chicken
> à la something concealed in a creamy mushroom
>   sauce in
> The Highwayman Suite . . .
> and when I pop to point Percy at
> the Porcelain . . .
> through the vestibule window . . .
> I see a horse-drawn carriage bearing
> *yet* another *whipped-creamed* bride
> and her *frock-coated* groom drawing
> up at the door for another
> Saturday wedding day . . .
> and all over . . .
> lots of two peoples are doing this thing
> and . . .
> they look so *young*
> and . . .
>
> *He struggles for . . .*

faces without . . .

faces clear of . . .

empty of . . .

He gets there . . .

stupid!

They all look . . . stupid . . .
their expressions   stupid
as if . . .
they have absolutely no idea at all why
they are doing what they are doing
who they are who she is who he is
what they've got on where they are
what they are promising to do
what it *means* . . . a wedding . . .

*Music . . . dramatic, 'something-wicked-this-way-
comes'-type soundtrack from* Casablanca *plays . . .*

Evelyn
Now.

Peter
What 'Now', darling?

Evelyn (*very politely*) Who are you?

A pause. Peter ceases being so tiddly.

Peter
Peter.
Your husband.

Evelyn
Who are you?

Peter
Your husband your husband your husband.

He's very tired . . .

I think I'll go and get out of these . . .

Have a shower.

Sandwich.

Would you like a sandwich, darling?

Evelyn gets up.

No. Don't get up.

I'm having a shower first.

She continues, moving towards him.

No.
No.
I'll just be upstairs.

She gets hold of his sleeve. Holds on.

No.
No, darling . . . Evelyn . . .

He tries to disengage her from his sleeve.

Evelyn (*distressed*)
Oh
oh
oh!

Peter
No!

Stay there.

Stay.
Evelyn . . .

Well come then.

Come on then.

Come.

Evelyn stretches out her hand to him. They move together as . . .

TWO
THE ENGAGEMENT

A woman, Sally, comes forward through the fog.
She smooths two dresses hanging up and tells us . . .

Sally
A wedding story.
Okay
I was at a reception . . .
naturally
Seating Plan had me
on the table where they put
all the Flotsam . . .
The Divorced, the Widowed
The Gay . . .
The Low-Marriage-Potential Crowd . . .
The Difficult-To-Slot-In-The-Big-World Brigade . . .
opposite and one across . . .
woman . . . my age . . .

Grace is seen . . .

thought she was straight on account of her shoes . . .
but
on the Flotsam Table so . . .
possibly she's . . . (*gay*)
Easy On The Eye . . .
and . . .
foreign! (*Oh, the Heaven Of It!*)

and . . .
to talk to . . . kind of . . . *larky* . . .

*Lot of repressed smiling and looking . . . very strong
immediate attraction. This is Romance!*

Grace
. . . Groom's mother's hat's *lovely*, isn't it . . .?

She's lying.

Sally
No.

Grace
Not a fan of the Sydney Opera House look?

Sally
I think it works as a public building . . .

Grace
. . . intersecting an expanse of sun-sparkling harbour
water . . .

Sally
yes . . . but I don't think it works on someone with
a face like
a smacked bum . . .

Grace
. . . you're saying my Auntie Lily has a face like a
smacked bum?

Sally
Oh. Dear.
I'm sorry.

Grace
No. You're really not. (*Pause.*)

Sally

Blown it.

Grace

You would have to smack a bum very hard
and very long to get it quite that . . . pink.

Sally

And I go . . . *that* pink!
Imagine!

Grace

Oh . . . Best Man's Speech!

Sally

Fuck!

Both listen.

Speech is very witty
Drinking references
Shagging references
Penis Penis Penis
her name's . . .

Grace

Grace.

Sally

Kind of a name's *that*?

Grace

From the Latin *gratia* apparently.
It means *grace* in the sense of the undeserved
favour of God . . .
Or the Greek *charis* . . .
to *rejoice* . . .

*They look at each other for a time. The Best Man's
speech starts up again as . . .*

Sally

    Marriage as . . . Prison Sentence
    Marriage as . . . Institution but who wants to live in an
    Institution? . . .
    Husband as . . . Innocent Victim
    Wife as . . . (*interestingly*) *Hitler*! . . .

    She looks at Grace. Grace equally interested . . .

    and then . . .
    but seriously
    Love
    Connubial Bliss . . .
    Commitment
    Sharing
    Security
    Togetherness
    on their long journey through Life . . .
    Ladies and Gentlemen
    The Bride and Groom!

    Champagne corks pop . . . cheering . . .

    Lot to drink
    Lot (*moving . . .*)
    Lot of covert, anti-wedding sniggering
    Lot
    with . . .

Grace

    Grace . . .

Sally

    and that in-class-no-laughing-at-the-back
    – throwback sensation
    activates my bladder into 'Go'
    and I'm in the Ladies . . .
    my senses are reeling . . .
    The Sentries At The Door In My Heart

are temporarily Off-Watch . . .
then she comes in . . .

Now they are in the Ladies as . . .

Ah. Grace. Rejoice.
Would you like to come into one of these
cubicles and   explore?

Grace
Outrageous.

Sally
Well. Forward. End Cubicle.
Come in here.
With me.

Grace
You are. Outrageous.

Sally
They expect Our Table to behave badly.
That's why they invite us to weddings.

Grace
My Auntie Lily invited me because she *hoped*
I'd meet a nice man . . .

Sally
Well . . . the night is young.
Coming?

Pause.

Grace
Hope to be.

They find this very funny . . . and they . . .

Sally
And we go together into the end cubicle . . .
it's the disabled one so it's got the most *space* . . .

To us . . .

Don't kid yourself . . .
A Wedding Story.
It always starts with Sex . . .

In the cubicle . . . sexy . . . but also funny . . .

Sally
Lock the door.

Grace
That'll mean we're Engaged.

This is very funny . . . they both laugh . . .

Sally
We can't hang about
every member of The Wedding
has been drinking for England . . .
The Men are peeing in The Rose Garden . . .
I sense Sydney Opera House
about to intersect the glittering expanse
of our Harbour of Love . . .
The Ladies Powder Room at
The Saracen's Head Hotel Bickley
is Ours Alone for but a moment . . .
. . . the younger bridesmaids
are pattering this way . . .

Speed Is Of The Essence . . .

Casablanca *soundtrack music as . . .*

. . . and there's locks and cramped spaces
and sanitary engineering
and fluids and U-bends and tissues
and getting cosmically caught with
passion pants down
Oh Brief and Fleeting Love!!!

Sally walks off leaving . . .

Grace
Well.
It'll make a good story!
'No . . . guess what *I* did once . . .!'
'At a *Wedding*'
'In *England*!'
So.
Phone Numbers. (*Exchanged.*)
She dances . . .
very badly . . .
with an oldish man . . .
then . . . (*Gesture for 'she goes'.*)

Sally and Peter come together . . . some appalling dancing . . .

Sally
I'll ring you!

Grace
'*Yeah . . . Right!*'
A Lift offer from . . . Sydney Opera House.
Sail off.
Sunset.

I'll just forget *all* about her!

Grace retires to forget all about her as . . .

THREE
TELLTALE STAINS

Peter (*matter of fact*)
She's stopped reading novels
your mother
since we retired.

Evelyn

I'm non-fiction.
Can't see the point of fiction.
Made-up stories.
I like facts
truth
details.
Fiction!
Well . . . who's got the *time*!

Peter

She wants to be with me all the time
your mother
arrange my day around her
sweet
bit of a second honeymoon actually . . .

Sally

'Sassy OAPs Enjoy Twilight Sex
Roguish Father Tells Queasy Daughter.'

Peter smiles at Sally. She smiles back . . .

Not a bad-tempered woman . . .
never a swearer . . .
fucking hell no . . .

Evelyn tuts slightly . . .

but . . .
started to become much more
abrupt

short fuse

fierce

and

these

small inexplicable moments of confusion . . .

Evelyn (*furious*)

> . . . I was there *fifteen* minutes early and
> Miss Busy-Reading-My-*Hello*-Magazine
> at Reception says 'Yes?'
> and I say 'Mrs Swan. Cut and Blow Dry at eleven-
> thirty'
> and she says 'We haven't got you down!' I said
> 'Tuesday the sixth at eleven-thirty . . .
> I made the appointment last time I was here.
> You wrote it down.'
> She says 'We've no record of it . . .'

Sally

> *She's* in 'A Cut Above' on Victoria Road,
> while in 'Hair Today!' on Halifax Avenue
> where she *has* made the appointment
> Shaznay trainee
> and Dale   stylist
> wait in vain . . .
> and driving with Evelyn
> just as   hairy

Peter

> Darling, what are you doing?

Evelyn (*furious*) . . .

> I'm just filling her with petrol and
> that . . . *man* . . . in the blue . . . *car* . . . just . . . calm as you
> like starts helping himself to the fuel thing *right* next
> door to me!
> The bloody *cheek*!
> The bloody damn *cheek* of it!
> I *slapped* his (*action for 'face'*) for him!!!
> The *bloody cheek*!

> *She sits down . . .*

Sally
> And then . . .
> and then one day . . .
> one *golden* evening . . .

Evelyn (*with great delight and warmth . . .*)
> Dolly and Jack
> *Tuxford* are coming for dinner!
> I haven't seen her since they lived in Mottisham
> and she's lost a *lot* of weight
> it's taken ten years off her!
> Wearing a *lovely* silk-knit top in a . . . you know the
> inside of an *oyster shell* . . .?

Peter
> *He's* still the same boring old gasbag . . .
> now doing an Open University on . . .

Evelyn/Peter
> Societal Constructs in Early Saxon Settlements . . .

Evelyn
> We start with my butternut squash and cinnamon
> soup . . .

Peter
> . . . served with the rest of the champagne . . .
> the Veuve Cliquot . . . well, we hadn't seen them for
> *years*!

They continue with parallel marital speaking . . .

Evelyn
> And then I'd just done lamb . . . because they're
> both quite *careful* eaters . . . but with some borlotti beans
> in a tomato garlicky sauce as well as vegetables . . . /
> broccoli . . . leeks
> roast potatoes   for the men

Peter (*speaking over from* /)
    I'd got a very nice red from
    my Wine Club . . . it was a Grand Cru . . . grenache
      grape . . .
    very nice . . .

Evelyn
    and a raspberry Pavlova . . .

Peter
    . . . very good Montrachet . . . and all the *chat* . . .

Evelyn
    No, no, no, Jack!
    All Your Early Saxon Societal Attitudes research
    is exactly the same as *my* modus operandi!
    You are looking for the *cause* of things
    Through the *effect* of things . . .
    For example
    For example
    There's a therosclerotic problem in the artery
    Causing infarction. Bang!
    A tumour!
    Ergo blood
    Ergo too much insulin
    Ergo too little glucose
    Ergo too little brain nutrition
    Ergo Coma! Bang!

Peter
    . . . shall I carve you a bit more lamb, Jack . . .?

Evelyn
    Sometimes, you examine the colon . . .
    Hmm . . . there's some post-op scar tissue and a
    Bit of intestine looped around it
    Ergo obstruction
    Ergo complication

Ergo distension
Ergo dehydration
Ergo vomiting

Peter
Dolly . . . bit more wine in your glass, my dear?

Evelyn
Blood!
Chemical Imbalance!
Arrythmia!
. . . a patient comes to a doctor
reveals one or two clues . . .
Bang!
Detective work begins

Peter
Darling, your sleeve is in your borlotti beans . . .

Evelyn lifts her wrist impatiently.

Evelyn
There are things we can see
There are things we can *find* out
Thus
Pathopsychology

Peter
Darling, you're *lecturing.*

Evelyn
Anything to stop Jack banging on about
Anglo-Saxon Settlements!
Ay, Dolly? . . . Dolly . . . have some more broccoli . . .
Jack, 'physiologia'
Greek root,
'an inquiry into the nature of suffering'.
Inquiry Jack . . .
'pathos'

suffering Dolly
put them together
you have it Bang! Doctors are Detectives!
Pursuing an inquiry into the nature of suffering . . .

Peter
Darling, you're *still* lecturing . . .

Evelyn
Well, I'm *tiddly* darling . . . I *always* lecture when I'm
tiddly . . .
Jack . . . Everything is about following the clues
Back
Back
Back
To the source and
Reconstructing the crime!
Find the perpetrator!
Counteract it with antidotes
Fortify the attacked victim . . . the organs!
Hold it in check
Until the body itself can fight back!
Have a strategy
Have a strategy
Jack

Peter
Evelyn . . .
I'm going to hit you with the leg of lamb if you
don't . . .

During the next speech, Evelyn gets the hiccups . . .

Evelyn
You see
A doctor
Is a fighter!
Is a soldier!

Who fights against his or her patients' . . .
Mortality
Jack . . .
Knowledge is
His or her armour . . . (*hic*)
Weapons
We need weapons . . . Dolly (*hic*)
Have some cream with that pavlova . . .
(*hic*) Peter . . .
(*hic*) can you get me a glass of (*hic*) water . . .?

Sally

Every, every illness . . .
we can fight . . .

*Evelyn drinks from the glass of water . . . cured of
hiccups as . . .*

her educated mind tells her
and she tells us

Peter

Can't get a word in *edgeways*!

Sally

Next morning . . .

Swirls of fog . . . dramatic Casablanca *music . . .*

Evelyn

What?

Who?

No.

Sally

Evelyn
can't remember any of it.

Peter

Jack!

Dolly!
Raspberry Pavlova!
Saxon Societal Constructs!
The Evelyn Swan Commemorative Lecture on
Pathophysiology!
The Hiccups!

Evelyn is completely mystified . . . disbelieving . . .

Sally

No amount of explanation can convince her
that Dolly and Jack had been there . . .

Evelyn

No.   No.   No.

Peter

Look! Dishwasher.
Four best dinner plates! . . . *four* red, *four* white wine
  glasses!
Four *flutes*!
For the champagne! £23.99 a bottle!
Look . . . bottom shelf of the fridge . . .
Remains of a *Leg of Lamb*!

Evelyn

I've no memory of it.
None.

*A pause. She looks at him. He looks away. Some mist
swirls. Then . . .*

Peter

Well. Sometimes I forget things too.
The champagne. Wine.
The excitement.
Maybe later.
She'll remember.
Maybe later.

Sally
　　Frightened Old Fucker.

　　She strokes her father's hair absent-mindedly, making
　　the parting sharp . . . She roots around in her pocket/
　　bag for a comb . . .

　　He almost convinces himself
　　that the whole thing
　　is
　　insignificant
　　as . . .

　　Finds instead . . .

FOUR
THE HONEYMOON

A piece of paper . . .

Sally
　　Her phone number
　　written on a piece torn off the
　　wedding breakfast menu . . .
　　I *really* wasn't . . .
　　it was just going to be one of those things . . .
　　(*Sings.*) 'just one of those crazy things . . .
　　a trip-to-the-moon-on-gossamer-wings . . .'
　　but my hands
　　quite independent of my brain
　　picked up the phone
　　dialled her number
　　and . . .
　　my body . . .
　　quite without permission from my intellect . . .
　　went off for a red-wine-intensive supper with her . . .

She is with Grace. It is the end of a long evening . . .
Sally is coming back from Grace's bathroom . . .

(*still to us*) That's Lust . . . isn't it?
I mean . . . that's not Love!

Grace
Okay?

Sally
Yes. Nice bathroom.

Grace
Well, it's not The Saracen's Head Bickley . . . but . . .

Sally
But then . . . where is?

They look at each other. Then . . .

Grace
Now.
Er.
Okay.
Look.
What happens now?
How do we go on with it? I mean . . . do we
go on with it . . . or was it just a fuck in a toilet
at a wedding? . . . because of course if we end
here that's fine it'll make a great competitive
bid in 'where's the weirdest place you've ever
fucked' conversations . . . I mean . . . (*furious*) I'm
always the first to do this! . . .
Look . . . I'm feeling
great *waves* of affection for you . . . and with
just a bit more I don't know . . . *reciprocity* from
you the waves of affection could become . . .

Sally
Reciprocity?

Grace
Isn't that a Word? . . . where you say back to me
'Yes . . . *I'm* feeling great waves of affection for *you* . . .'

Sally
Ripples . . . I've got ripples . . .

Grace
How you are in the first three weeks
is how you'll be for the rest of the relationship . . .
I'm feeling waves you're feeling ripples . . .
It's doomed.

Evelyn (*to us*)
Has someone been in this cupboard?
Everything's been moved round!

Sally
Grace . . .

Grace
Yes?

Sally
You say 'Come into my bedroom and see
if we can capture the majesty and grandeur
of that first time in the Saracen's Head Hotel Bickley
Ladies Powder Room cubicle . . .'

Grace (*in French*)
Come into my bedroom and see if we
can capture / the majesty and grandeur of
that first time in the Saracen's Head Hotel Bickley
Ladies Powder Room cubicle . . .

Sally (*as Grace repeats /*)
I haven't got time for this!
I haven't got the energy!
I know this . . . this is the *honeymoon*!
This is the easy bit!

the being in bed in the daytime bit . . .
the Swooning ! . . .

Peter

You see . . . (*lecturing*)
the *medieval* concept of Love . . .

> Thus possed to and fro
> Al stereless within a boot am I
> Amydde the see, betwixen wyndes two,
> Thet in contrarie stonden evere mo,
> Allas, what is this wondre maladie?
> For hote of cold, for cold of hote, I die.

From Chaucer . . . look at *The Knight's Tale* . . .
Petrarch, Dante . . . through Wyatt . . . Spenser . . .
even, I *suppose*, Shakespeare . . .
Rosalind . . . *As You Like It* . . . says
'Love is merely a madness, and I tell you,
deserves as well a dark house and a whip
as madmen do; and the reason why they are
not so punished and cured is that the lunacy
is so ordinary that the whippers are in love too . . .'
. . . was that it was *an illness*!
that you *caught*.

Sally

Yes, Dad.

Peter

You became *not* yourself . . .

Sally

Dad!

Grace

That man . . . at the wedding . . .
who you danced rock'n'roll with?
Was that your father?

Sally is embarassed . . .

Sally
That was my father, yes. But that
wasn't me.

Evelyn (*to us*)
Somebody's been wearing my shoes!

Grace
Your mother   is she . . .
around . . .?

FIVE
AN IMMACULATE WAISTBAND

. . . which is a familiar family recounting of . . .

Sally
Peter Swan
met Evelyn Phyllis Roderick
when she was
nineteen and he was twenty-one . . .

She cues her mother in . . .

'I was wearing . . .'

Evelyn
. . . I was wearing a navy blue crepe dress

*Evelyn is fully compos mentis. It is some time earlier.
Sally mimics her mother's precise hand movements
with affectionate scorn as . . .*

with pin tucks under the bust . . .
and a skirt cut on the bias so it . . .

Sally/Evelyn
swirled in a *perfect* circle when I danced . . .

Evelyn dances. Sally joins her. Evelyn is a very good dancer. Peter watches . . .

Peter
She looked lovely. She looked lovely!

Evelyn breaks off dancing as . . .

Evelyn
. . . and he was in a corduroy suit!
I'd never seen a corduroy *suit* before!

Sally
What were the trousers like, Mum?

Both women continue their delicate hand movements as . . .

Evelyn
Beautifully cut.
Plenty of material falling with pleats
from an *immaculate* waistband . . .

Sally continues the precise hand movements over the next speech, which makes Evelyn smile . . .

Sally
. . . so you couldn't see how *packed* his
lunchbox was . . . you could only speculate
as to the size and *magnificence* of his fishing tackle
. . you
couldn't get your loop out and study the
treasure trove that was his family jewels . . .

Evelyn slaps Sally playfully hard on wrist. A mother's slap.

Evelyn
Oh, you didn't know anything about that side of things /

Peter
/ you *tried*. Got you nowhere.

Evelyn
till you were married . . .

Sally
. . . which they duly were at . . .

Sally/Evelyn
St Christopher's Church, Peel Lane, Ottisford . . .
fourteenth of May . . .
a *lovely* day for it . . .

Evelyn
. . . my dress was a heavy shantung silk . . . floor-length
with a demi-monde train . . . edged at the bodice, cuffs
and hem with *tiny* tear-drop ersatz pearls . . .

Sally is mouthing and miming occasionally . . .
fondly . . . laconically . . .

Peter
. . . I turned to see her come down the aisle . . .
and . . . my eyes filled with tears, Sally . . .
I had to turn and look up at the *ceiling* . . .
make the tears drop back in . . .

To blink them back . . .

Evelyn
. . . we had the reception at The Bunch of Grapes,
Mottingham . . . and everybody was lovely apart
from that doctor friend of your cousin Anne's . . .
with the black tongue from all that red wine
and the food stains all over her blouse
and the *language* . . .
what was she called?

Peter
Ivy Vickerman?

Evelyn (*absolute contempt for this suggestion*)
No!

37

No!
No!!!

A long pause . . .
   Evelyn realises she must be very clear in dealing
with these very stupid people . . .

. . . the one in the grey pinstripe costume . . .
with the fox-fur . . . and cloche hat . . . *black* cloche
   hat! . . .

To Sally:

She was sitting next to *you* . . . right next to *you* . . .
what was she called? . . .

A pause . . .

Sally
   I don't know, Mum.
   I wasn't there.

Evelyn (*to Peter . . . huge, revolted vehemence*)
   That's right!
   Get your *fucking cunting girlfriend* to come and *lie*
      to me!

Sally
   Dad . . .

Peter
   No.

   No!!!!!!

   Sally picks up a dress on a hanger. Shows it to Evelyn.

Sally
   What d'you think of this, Mum?

   Evelyn approves and recognises . . .

Evelyn
Oh!
That's *kingfisher* blue, isn't it?

Sally/Evelyn
It's blue with green sort of *underneath* . . .

SIX
AND THEN THERE'S COURTING . . .

Sally (*to us*)
. . . And then
there's *courting* . . .
giving your presents . . .

Grace comes to her, incredulously holding . . .

Grace
A whoopee cushion?

Sally
A Design Comedy Classic . . .
I was in a shop by the British Museum and . . .

She mimes seeing it by surprise . . .

you have to blow air into it . . .
like this . . .

She kisses Grace deeply on the lips . . .

Grace (*singing*)
'. . . take my breath away . . .'

(*and*) '. . . up, up and away . . .
in my beautiful balloon . . .'

As Grace blows air into it . . .

Sally

The bits of you you take and give to them
you're so *generous* when
you're courting . . .
'Here's my *best* bits . . .
I'm *Adorable*' . . .
Okay, now you put it on a chair
and somebody sits down on it . . .

*Grace puts the whoopee cushion on the chair . . . then
walks away . . . walks back as . . .*

and . . .
you're on your absolutely *best* behaviour . . .
because you want this person who you
like to like you even *more* . . .
so the romance the fever the illness
the madness continues to
invade your senses . . .

Grace sits down on the whoopee cushion . . .

Sally

What d'you think?

Grace

It's *so* romantic.

Sally

You can make it do different ones . . .
depending on the pressure you . . .

Grace (*as Sally blows it up again*)

. . . so
it's not just the one magical experience then . . .?

Sally

Oh no.
It's like multiple orgasms . . .
(*to us*) and Courting's when you get to tell all your
stories . . .

To Grace, as Grace experiments with the different
sounds you can get out of a whoopee cushion . . .

I got one in my stocking one Christmas . . .
and Mum and Dad were *Princely* about
the number of times
one would sit on it . . .
and . . .

Whoopee cushion farts . . .

Evelyn
Peter . . . was that rude noise *you*?

Sally
and then I'd put it on *her* chair
and he'd be like . . .

Whoopee cushion farts . . .

Peter
Evelyn!
Did you have too many baked beans
yesterday?

Sally laughing . . .

Sally
And they were *Stars*
totally surprised
every time
all Christmas Day
then
Boxing Day morning
I put it on Mum's chair
and it's . . .

Farting noise again . . .

Evelyn
Alright, I think we've had enough of that, Sally!

Sally pauses, five-year-old face, body, invades her . . .

Sally
Fucker.
Fucking Tricky Fucker!
Gives . . . then . . . Takes it Away!

Grace
Have you told her about me?

Sally
well . . .   no.
(*To us.*) Why should I?
Not going to be permanent, this.
This is just a . . . diversion . . .
Well . . . live in the moment, right?
and anyway . . .

SEVEN
IN SICKNESS AND IN HEALTH

Peter picks up a golf trophy . . . is dusting it as Evelyn comes in.

Evelyn
What are doing?

Peter
Dusting, darling.

Danger-approaching music plays. Evelyn very paranoid . . . therefore very dangerous suddenly . . .

Evelyn
What are you doing in my house?
What are you doing with my husband's things?

Peter
It's my golf trophy. Look.
Peter Swan. Hazel Dene Golf Clu . . .

Evelyn
Those are my husband's golf trophies.

She goes to him, wrestles the trophy from his hands . . .

Evelyn
Give that to me!
Steal from my house!!!

She starts to break things, throw things at him . . .

I'm calling my daughter!
Tell her what you're doing!

She dials.

Sally!
There's a man here stealing Daddy's things!

Sally
Where's Daddy, Mum?

Evelyn
I don't know!
There's just this man!

Sally
Put him on, Mum.
Put that man on, Mum.
I'll talk to him.

Evelyn
My daughter wants a word with you!

Peter
Sally . . .

Sally
Dad.

Pause. An awful moment.

What's she doing?

Peter
She's . . .

Peter is savagely attacked by Evelyn. He is still. Sally listens.

Evelyn (*same time as . . .*)
Thief! Robber! Steal . . .?
Steal? Steal? Doesn't belong to you!
That's my husband's!

Peter (*same time as Evelyn*)
Evelyn . . .
Evelyn . . . it's me . . . it's Peter . . . Peter . . .
Evelyn . . .

Sally
Dad.
Get out of there.
Leave the house right away.
I'm calling the police . . .

Peter
Police came. Patrol car!
Right smack front of the house . . .! (*the disgrace*)

Evelyn
He's not my husband.
Come with me.
I'll show you a picture of my husband!

Photo still of Peter and Evelyn's wedding . . .

Peter
The policeman's *Jack* from the Golf Club!
Five par.
Says . . .
'This man looks like your husband,
standing right here . . .'

Evelyn
He's *not* my husband!

Peter
Denise came in from next door . . .

Evelyn
Denise . . .!

Peter
Denise said, 'Evelyn, you know I love you
and I wouldn't lie to you.
This man is Peter . . .
turn around and look.'
and she did just as she was told . . .

Evelyn turns round. Sees Peter . . . as if for the first time . . .

Evelyn
Peter!
Oh, thank God you're here!
Somebody's been in here trying to
steal your golf trophies!!!

Sally
Fucking Drama Queen.

Evelyn
Sally!

Sally
I'm living about two hundred miles away
but . . .

She goes towards Evelyn, who . . .

EIGHT
WHAT ONCE I WAS . . .

*. . . greets Sally with great love. Sally sits Evelyn down
with her . . .*

Sally
What's Alzheimer's Disease, Mum?

Evelyn
Well, love . . . The fundamental pathology of
Alzheimer's Disease
is the progressive degeneration and loss
of vast numbers of nerve cells in those portions
of the brain's cortex that are associated with
the so-called higher functions,
such as
memory
learning
judgement.

Looks to see if Sally is taking it in . . .

Sally
Mmm.   Fuck.

Evelyn slaps Sally lightly for swearing.

memory
learning
judgement.

*Evelyn looks at Sally's hair in a 'it-won't-do' motherly
way . . . as . . .*

Evelyn
The severity and nature of the patient's dementia
at any given time are proportional to the number and
location of cells that have been affected.

She starts tidying Sally's hair as . . .

Evelyn
The decrease in nerve-cell population is in itself
sufficient to explain the memory loss and other
cognitive disabilities, but there is another factor
that seems to play a role as well . . .
this needs a good haircut . . .
a marked decrease in acetylcholine . . .
the chemical used by these cells
to transmit messages . . .
am I lecturing, darling?

Sally
Oh yes.

Sally takes Evelyn's hand in hers . . .

(*To us.*) Here's the dreadful irony . . .
Evelyn is a doctor . . .
was a doctor . . .?

Evelyn
These are the basic elements of what we know
about Alzheimer's . . .

She turns over Sally's hands . . .

You need to spend some time on your nails, lady . . .

The long lists of cause, effects, treatments
in other illnesses
have no analogy to the present state of
our knowledge . . .
or ignorance . . .
of Alzheimer's.
We know not a whit more
about what might cure it
than we do about what might cause it.

I've got it   haven't I?

Sally
Yes, Mum.

Evelyn
Oh Sally.

*She sees she has Sally's hand in hers. She grips it
tightly. Fog plays around their feet as . . .*

With the kingfisher blue . . .
My *dark* navy court shoes.
Not the black.
Not the black!

NINE
THE MIDDLE OF THE NIGHT

Sally
And
in the middle of the night . . .

Darkness on all but Sally's face . . . we hear . . .

Peter
What?
Evelyn
What are you doing here?
Since when?
Since when?
Since When?????
Does a brother sleep with his sister?
You're disgusting!
Get out of here!
Out!
Out, you incestuous bastard!

*Light widens to reveal Peter standing at the edge of
Sally's space . . .*

48

Sally
How long has this been going on?

Peter
It's not all the time.
I come down and sleep on the . . .

Sofa bed, where Sally is . . . both listen as . . .

Evelyn (*absolute hate*)
I won't have it
I won't have it
I will not have it!
(*to us*) Who do they think they *are*???
the thing is
I feel just . . .

*She can't find the word 'fine' . . . only the smile and
the body attitude . . .*

Look at me
we do walks every weekend
I'm more (*fit*) than most of the
younger women in . . .

She can't find the word for Aerobics Class . . . acts it . . .

up down . . . what you
wear . . . (*leotard . . .*)
Peter and I   we still
it's not *exciting* any more
it's *comfortable*   but
we still   most weeks
manage   a bit of a
quite *athletic* . . .

Can't find . . . 'cuddle' . . . 'sex' . . .

with . . . *willy*! . . . that thing . . .

I've looked after myself!

It

Oh dear

you lose . . .

I don't want strangers wiping my . . . (*what?*)

I think if I talk to Fitzpatrick . . .
get him to give me a diet sheet
keep exercising my . . .

Can't find . . . 'mind', acts it . . .

keep . . .
we'll be . . .

you see
Peter's not much of a . . .
it's not his strength . . .
and (*points to Sally . . . what is her name?*)
well . . . she's got her own life to . . .
and . . . (*can't remember*) . . . someone . . .

She looks to where . . .

TEN
SOMEONE

Somewhere in the fog, Robin appears.

Robin (*as Bogart*)
    'Of all the
    gin joints in all the towns
    in all the world . . .
    she comes into my gin joint . . .'

Evelyn (*utter joy*)
    Oh!

Robin performs excellent impersonation of Dooley Wilson . . . Evelyn as Ingrid.

Ingrid
Hello Sam . . .

Dooley
Hello Miss Elsa.
I never expect to see you again.

Ingrid
Yes, it's been a long time.

Dooley
Yes Ma'am, a lot of water under the bridge.

Ingrid
Some of the old songs, Sam

Dooley
Yes Ma'am.

Piano music from Casablanca *plays under . . .*

Evelyn (*enchanted*)
Yes!

Robin as . . .

Ingrid
Play it once, Sam. For old time's sake.

Dooley
I don't know what you mean, Miss Elsa.

Ingrid (*whisper*)
Play it Sam. Play 'As Time Goes By'.

Dooley
Oh, I cain't remember it, Miss Elsa . . .
I'm a li'l rusty on it . . .

Evelyn laughs, claps as . . .

Ingrid
> I'll hum it for you . . .
> da day day day day da
> da day day day day day da . . .

Evelyn is in Heaven as . . .

Dooley
> You must remember this . . .

Sally sings it quietly as . . .

Bogart
> I thought I told you never to play
> that song again, Sam . . .

The soundtrack score after Bogart's interruption plays as . . .

Evelyn
> More!

Fog envelops him as Evelyn, we see, is crying . . .

> Who are you?
> Who are you?

> I'll talk to Fitzpatrick about care
> . . . where we stand financially . . .
> I've sent patients to council places that are
> *perfectly* . . .

She thinks . . .

> perfectly . . .

Laughs ruefully . . .

> Rows of *frightful* chairfuls of old . . .

Can't find 'women'.

> That'll teach you . . .

Do As You Would Be Done By . . .

Can't remember her name . . .

Now . . .
Who are you . . .? (*No idea.*)

I'll be alright
I'll be alright
It'll all be alright! (*She's convinced.*)

Peter?
Peter?

She keeps calling his name over . . . as . . .

Sally (*to Peter*)
She can't stay with you.
We have to find somewhere for her.
Somewhere *safe*.
Don't we?
Don't we?

ELEVEN
IN SICKNESS AND IN HEALTH . . .

Sally
Well . . . this is where he should say . . .

Peter
I can look after her.
I'd like to do that.
Look after her.
It'll be alright.

Sally
Well . . .
He married her . . .
He promised to love honour and all that

until Death Do Them Part!
It's Down To Him!
But he doesn't.
He just says . . .

Peter

I'm tired.

Find somewhere for her.

Just for . . .

Yes.

Sally

Of course, this is the moment
I should step in . . .
say
'*I'm* not married.
I've no family of my own . . .
I'll take care of her . . .'
But I don't . . . it's not how we do it these days . . .

Peter

I still love your mother.
But . . .

He bursts into tears . . .

Sally

Well, I'm not having this!
No!
What happened to Courtly Love, Professor Swan?
Parfit gentil fucking knight, Dad!
This isn't in my contract.
I'm *The Daughter*!
I'm *The One Who Gets Looked After*!
I'm *The One Who GETS AWAY WITH MURDER*!
She's The *Parent*!
He's The Parent!

Children looking after Parents!
When did *that* start?
I've had no choice in all this . . .
I'm getting on with my own life!
I've constructed a whole network of intricate
dysfunctional relationships of my own to
mismanage I can't drop all that and buy into this
fucking . . . *Chechnia*!
fucking . . . *Kosovo*!
fucking . . . *Holocaust*!
I haven't . . . *Time* . . . for this because . . .
to get back to *my* life . . .
because . . .
a fucking *flanker* attack!

TWELVE
THE PROPOSAL

*She walks into the end of a long discussion about 'where
is our relationship going . . .?'*

Grace
I want to be married.
I want to be married. To you.

Sally
Agghh. Grace! Grace!
Why? Why? Why?

Grace
I love you. I want to be with you for ever.

Sally
Agh! Don't hold back. Say what you mean . . .

Grace
And I want a public acknowledgement of it
. . . Like everybody else.

Sally
Oh please God . . . not *politics* . . .

Grace
It's a simple human right . . .

Sally
Getting a bit edgy getting a bit queasy all getting
a bit Marge Piercy a bit early Feminism and
late religious and *awful* marriage of concepts
I mean
It's not as if we'll have children . . . (*Big mistake* . . .)

Grace
We might.
We might.
It's the year 2000. It's possible. People do it.
Why not?

A phone rings . . . lights up gradually on . . . Robin . . .

Sally (*phone to Robin*)
It's like one of those dodgy fucking
low-budget independent lesbian films . . .
She said, 'Let's get married.'

Robin (*mock-serious voice*)
'Well,
technically, that's not possible in the United Kingdom . . .'

Sally
She'll get some fucking *Dane* shipped over.
Or we'll have to go to fucking *Amsterdam*!
She said 'Let's have children.'

Robin (*ditto*)
'Well, biologically, that's not possible'

Sally
The fucking Turkey Baster Road . . .

Robin (*queasy*)
Feeling a bit faint now . . .

Sally
I became a lesbian to get out of all that . . .

Robin (*ditto*)
'Well, our research intimates that
you became a lesbian because of a homosexual
gene which means it is neither *your* fault nor
the fault of your tragically disappointed parents . . .'

Sally
How's the weather in Berkeley?

Robin
In the seventies . . .

Sally
Fuck you.

Robin
I'm missing seasons.
Fuck you.

How's Evelyn . . .?

*Sally is back with Grace. The lighting is all bars . . .
impressionistic prison as . . .*

Sally (*to Grace . . .*)
. . . I can't do this now.
Shall we not talk about it tonight?
Can we wait? . . . Seem to be in waiting mode just at
the moment . . .?
I don't know if I can ever do it.
I feel sick.
The whole idea makes me queasy.
It's a health thing.
I need to look after myself.

Be unfaithful a lot.
Carry a big inhalant of . . . freedom. Just In Case.
Is it stuffy in here?
Place is full of smoke!
No air.

. . . Can we open the window?

Escape.

A plane flies over . . .

THIRTEEN
AN AIRPORT HEAD

Robin, waiting at an airport . . .

Robin
Need something to read on the plane . . .
being my mother's son . . .
do the research
know what you're talking about
(*Quoting.*) 'facts
truth
details . . .
I mean . . . *Fiction?*
well, who's got time?'
I go for factual . . .
(*Reads.*) . . . 'The single most important one is
a stark statistic . . . Alzheimer's disease strikes more
than 11 per cent of the population over sixty-five . . .
by the year 2030, the population over sixty-five
will reach 60 million or more . . .
The magnitude of the problem is staggering . . .'

Takes it in and . . .

And . . .

. . . alchemises it.

a great premise for a *film* scenario . . .
It's 2030. The Near Future.
The Young . . . among them . . . DiCaprio . . .
live in digitally-created fortress cities.
Outside the walls . . . in the wild country . . .
The Old . . . the Dangerously Forgetful . . .
played by a host of veteran actors . . . Dames of
the British Theatre . . . Maggie Smith . . . Diana Rigg . . .
plucky little Judi Dench . . . roam about . . .
helped and fed only by a small band of
caring Robin Hood types . . .
led by a tough, sassy, leather-clad . . . Julia Roberts.
She breaks into DiCaprio's electronically-surveillance-
protected apartment to steal food and supplies . . .
Maggie, Diana and Judi are in the forest,
scene-grabbingly warming their gnarled hands
at a glowing fire . . .
DiCaprio catches Judi . . . her hands in the ice-box . . .
and his cold, Look-Out-For-Number-One
philosophy is challenged when, having fallen in love
with her . . . life-brightening laugh and tough honesty . . .
he defends her against a pack of rabid OAPs.
She's a Star, but she's also a Woman
and finally, she's no match on her own against The Old.
It's a love story that plugs into the Zeitgeist.

Awful reality swirls around him as . . .

(*He returns to reading . . .*) 'Typically . . .
the disease is slowly
but relentlessly progressive . . .
it usually leads to death in about seven to ten years . . .
but it can progress more quickly . . .

say three to four years . . .
or
it can take as long as fifteen . . .'

*He stares out of the window. The plane continues to
fly as . . .*

Well shit.

(*as Bogart*) 'But what happens to us three
small people
don't amount to a hill of beans
in this
crazy world . . .'

*He watches the crazy world below him as . . . music . . .
perky version, with table-banging of 'Knock on Wood'
from* Casablanca *as . . .*

FOURTEEN
THE HIT

*Peter is trying to do a crossword. He is exhausted.
Evelyn is wondering/wandering about . . . he has to
watch her as she wanders . . . in case she encounters
danger to herself . . . or to others. Music underplays,
irritatingly cheery . . .*

Evelyn
    Ah!

Peter
    I'm tired.
    Don't do that.
    Don't do that . . . you'll . . .

    Oh, God . . . *See?*

He brings her back to him. She stands. He sits.

Just five minutes . . .
Five minutes while I do my crossword . . .
Try.
Twenty-three across. 'Variegated pepper used to get
rid of rats.' Five–four.
I think it might be an anagram of . . .
No
no
no!
You watch . . .
watch then . . .

Evelyn
Oh.

She wanders off again . . .

Peter
You play with . . .
you just sit and . . . just for a *minute* . . .

She wanders. He fetches her back.

one minute

She wanders off again.

Evelyn
Ah!

Peter
No!

*Peter goes to Evelyn, stands quivering for a minute,
then he punches her hard . . . She looks at him . . .
looks at her arm . . . slowly puts a hand to where she
was hit. Her face is surly . . . she cowers minutely, like
a dog that has been beaten . . .*

FIFTEEN
HOME

Robin comes in . . . Duty-free bag. Flight bag. Books.

Robin
Home.

INTERIOR. DAY.
We are in an institutional building.
It's unbearably grim.
In long shot . . .
we see an expensively-dressed man
Hugo Boss suit.   (*No we don't.*)
Flight bag. Duty-free carrier bag.
Books.
Character notes . . . successful, highly intelligent . . .
but with a slightly dangerous *edge*.
Standing end of long long corridor.
Lighting is expressionistic.
Max Reinhardt.
Close-up on his face.
Bars effect.
Face is haunted.
Bleak.
Semiotic suggestion of . . . Prison.

He looks around . . .

For £650 a week.
Very clean . . . but . . .
Christ! . . .
Voice-over reveals what he is thinking.
Jackbooted prison guard frogmarches past.
Protagonist speaks.

To someone . . . a nice nurse . . .

Doctor Swan?
Mrs Swan?
Evelyn Phyllis Swa . . .
Evelyn . . .

Listens with polite attention as he is told . . .

You're known by your *first* name here . . .
it's friendly . . . you see . . .

Large notice board says
'Today is Wednesday. The weather is sunny'

Listens with polite attention as he is told . . .

It's our Orientation Chart.
It *Helps.*

Walks into . . .

Hello, Mum.

Evelyn looks his way.

It's me.

Robin!

Evelyn's face breaks into a huge welcoming smile.

Mum . . .

Evelyn
I love you!
You're so handsome!
I love you!

*She puts her arms round him and they hug and kiss
ecstatically, both crying . . .*

Robin
I feel so *loved*!

Evelyn intensely loving . . .

Evelyn
Darling!
Darling!

I love you!

Robin
I love you too.

Crosscut to door.
A nurse.
Protagonist expects Mother to
proudly introduce prodigal son
but . . .

Seeing Nurse . . .

Evelyn
I love you!
You're so beautiful.
And I love you!

Robin
The nurse is as loved.

He leaves as . . . Evelyn continues to say . . .

Evelyn
I love you!
You're beautiful.
I love you!
Darling!

Sally
And Peggy the Cleaner and Ollie the Cleaner
and the Egg Lady
and Ronnie the Health Visitor.
The man from Granada who is mending the
new ward TV.
She's suddenly Dazzlingly Unfaithful

Love The One You're With!
Forget Courtly Love, Dad.
We've accelerated into The Sixties!
Everything is a First Date!
Once
she even says it to me!

Robin into . . .

Robin
Dad!

Robin and Peter hug and shake hands, manly . . .

Just been to see her . . .

Peter puts his hand on Robin's arm . . . distressed . . .

Peter
I went and dragged her back . . .
and I rammed her back in her seat . . .
and . . .
when I sat down . . .
with my onside hand . . .
my secret   concealed   hand

I
punched her

He demonstrates to Robin . . .

right in her side
on purpose

Robin
Dad.

Peter
on *purpose*

I wanted to   really   *hurt* her

He cries.

Robin
She hit you once . . .
I saw her . . . when you were dancing
in the garden with Mrs Hall . . .

Peter (*still crying*)
. . . but I *deserved* that . . .!

Robin
Dad
people *hit*.
It's not the end of the world.

Peter
I'm at the end of my tether, son.

SIXTEEN
SIBLINGS

Sally arrives to Robin . . .

Sally
Okay.
Enough.
I'd like my mum back now.

Robin
Yeah.
The real one.
This *Invasion of the Bodysnatchers* thing.
Not working for me.

Sally
The real one. With all her loveable faults.

Robin
Even with *all* her loveable faults?

Sally (*pause*)
Yes.

Robin
Okay. Plus the *real* Dad.

Sally
Not that decrepit old imposter

Peter
I heard that!

Robin
I'm not grown-up enough for this.
I look sophisticated and handsome but actually I'm
only *six*.

Sally
Me too.
I've got my hanky tucked in my knickers.

Robin
And my mittens on elastic through the sleeves of my
coat.

Sally
I'm actually not old enough to do my own coat buttons
up.

Robin
And somebody's still got to cut up my food.

Sally
We weren't told.

Robin
It's an outrage expecting two *tiny children* like us to
cope with this!

Sally
It's abuse.

Robin
Yes.
Ring a Child Help Hotline.

A pause.

Sally
Give me a big American kind of hug.

Robin (*doing so*)
Actually . . . *you're* the oldest . . . you
should . . .

Sally
No . . . *I* boss . . . *you* do what I say. Our kid.

Robin
And I *am* the man.

Sally
True.

They hold one another tight . . .

You do everything. Sort it out. Cope.

Robin
Okay.

Pause.

Well, fuck, what can we do?

Casablanca *music* . . .

Robin/Sally (*dramatic voice-over voice*)
            but wait
            and wait

    and wait . . .

SEVENTEEN
WAITING, WAITING, WAITING . . .

Peter is sitting . . .

Peter (*to Robin*)
It's a good idea to sit out
occasionally . . . with all the others . . .
wives   husbands

children come when they can, obviously . . .

it's the family comes mainly

. . . quite useful . . . informative to swap stories . . .
exchange strategies and just talk to someone who . .
   (*understands*)

it's a good idea to bring a book because . . .
   (*it's so boring*)

Nothing much to say really
sometimes we all just sit and cry . . .
worse than . . . Rolf Harris . . . *Animal Hospital* . . .
what a business . . .

*Sally sits down too. Robin roams about . . . Peter
reading . . .*

Sally
So.
California?

Robin
Sunny.
Money.
Funny.

Peter
How's the Work?

Robin
Tiptop, Dad.
Very hard. Very intense. Very challenging.

Sally
Still 'in love' with it?

Robin
Passionately.
Nagy-Wellcome Lecture.

Sally
On?

Robin
Structure and Image Systems of . . .

Sally
Casablanca . . .

Peter
Your mother's favourite film . . .

Sally/Robin (*mock amazement*)
No?????

Peter (*quoting badly*)
. . . 'Play it again, Sam . . .'

Sally/Robin exchange glances of pity and derision . . .

Robin
It isn't actually '*again*' . . . Dad . . . it's just . . . 'Play It,
Sam . . .'

Sally puts a hand on his arm, shakes her head . . .
   They all wait . . . Robin comes and sits close to
Sally.

Robin (*whispering, furious*)
He can quote the whole
of English Literature from *Gammer Gurton's Needle*

to *Rape of The Lock* . . . but he can't watch a fucking
film with proper *attention* . . .

Sally (*fairly good impersonation from* . . .)
Liebchen . . .

Robin (*perfect impersonation from* Casablanca)
. . . here speaking American for practice . . .

Sally
. . . darling sweetheart head . . .
What watch?

Robin (*looking at his watch*)
Ten watch. (*Sighs.*)

Waits . . .

Sally
Love life?

Robin
Nada.

Sally
Sex life?

Robin
Panda.
You?

Grace appears . . . it is earlier . . .

Grace
I called.
Your ansaphone.

Left a message.
You'll call when you get in, I thought.
I leave another message.
I'll be reading in bed.
Call me when you get in.

Three o'clock I wake up. . . .
This is so humiliating and clichéd.
My brain's turning into some kind of *Chocolate*!
Beginning to get the picture here
beginning to understand the subtext . . .
I lie in bed arguing with myself that you've
got in but you were too *drunk* to listen
to your messages or you're too *nice* to wake
me up so late but I *know* you're not that nice
you're somewhere
Making Whoopee
Hay
Creating . . . *Schism* . . . no matter how I argue
against myself on your behalf . . . for your sweet
nature for your loving constancy
I know that although there's no *phone*
message from you there's one Big Cosmic
Message . . .

*Grace swears to herself fulsomely in her own language
as light on her fades into . . .*

Sally
We're on a break.

Not liking it. Robin sees. Face and body sympathise . . .

Why?

*Grace and Sally, from their separate places, conduct
a parallel rant at each other . . .*

Sally
I've got a lot to deal with, alright?

Grace
I *know*.
But.
Time's Wingèd Chariot.
I love you.

72

Sally

Ugh. Don't. Don't.

Grace looks.
    In parallel . . . big big rant . . .

Grace

You know what . . .
I think you're right . . .
It might not work.
I mean . . . we don't want to endure the
heart-rending embarrassment of a *perverse* ceremony
do we? No!
I mean . . . we have to look ahead!
Expect disaster!
Keep a lookout for *problems*!
I mean . . . the future can only be *bleak*, yes?
I mean . . . you might *get ill* . . .
I might get ill . . . Ah! . . . so no point
getting into anything when people might get *ill*!

Sally

Love! What's that? Free care!
Custodial! Regulations.
And . . . Bother!
And *two* people like . . . *coupled*
like a . . . *chain* . . . chains! . . . it's
concave . . . not . . . convex . . .
looks *in*
not   *out*
can that be the way to . . .?
shouldn't it . . . *free* . . .?
not . . . tie *down* . . . pin *down* . . .
'Let the winds of Heaven blow between you!'
Rejoice in what we've got!
Grace!
Rejoice!

73

Can't it . . . we . . . stay?
Doesn't doing something to . . . *fix* it . . .
Change it?

Until . . .

I don't understand you!

Grace
I understand you.
I understand you.
Coward.

Sally
There's few things to . . . (*She mimes ironing* . . .)

Robin takes her hand. Looks at it . . .

Robin
Your hands are getting just like . . . Mum's.

*Sally tries to take her hand away. Robin resists.
A slapping match. Funny. It subsides.*

Sally
Heard from Julie?

Robin
Christmas.

Sally
How's Tom and Sophie?

*Robin takes some photographs out of his wallet . . .
hands them one by one to Sally . . .*

Robin
Good . . . good.

Sally
This is still in Greece . . .?

Robin
Kalkidiki . . .

Sally

So she's still with . . . Costas?

Robin

No. But that's okay, apparently.

Sally

Well . . . they're nice and brown, anyway . . .

Robin

As soon as they can . . .
He's twenty . . . she's eighteen . . .
they become more and more curious
about me . . .
they track me down . . .
I'm older but well-preserved.
Kevin Costner's playing me.

Sally

Nice.
But he'll never capture your
impenetrable depths . . .

Robin shrugs . . .

Robin

It's heart-stopping at first . . .
that moment when they come upon me . . .
de-barnacling my seagoing boat . . .
and there's many individual and group
scenes where they hurl recriminations
and hurt at my head . . .

Sally

But you keep a gritty silence about their
mother's behaviour . . . because under that
craggy, beachbum exterior . . . you're a
gentleman . . .

Robin

And . . . slowly . . . achingly . . . they soften
towards me . . .

Sally

they want a ride on the fucking boat . . .

Robin

first . . . the girl . . .
then . . . oh so reluctantly . . .
the boy . . .

Sally

They love him in the end.

Robin nods. Sally puts her arms round him.

Waves crash.
Seagulls.
Magnificent sunset . . .

EIGHTEEN
A MAGNIFICENT SUNSET

Peter washes Evelyn's face with a flannel as . . .

Peter

Darling
We need to discuss something . . .
I've   put the house on the market . . .

*Evelyn responds only to the ministrations of the
flannel . . .*

Evelyn

Erf . . .

Peter

Well   it's   the size
and the money freed up would be handy for . . .

He indicates 'all this' . . .

and
there's a flat I've had a look at . . .

Evelyn
  Na . . .

Peter
  Very handy for the A437 so I
  can zoom up here in twenty-three minutes
  in decent traffic density . . .
  Cliveden Road   so
  and   view over the eighth and ninth greens!
  You've always said I live at the bloody Golf
  Club anyway . . .
  anyway
  I've talked it over with those two
  and
  well, Robin's not keen but you know how he
  loves that house . . . but Sally thinks go for it . . .

Evelyn
  Bucket!

Peter
  Make everything . . .
  easier to manage
  efficiency-wise
  for whatever happens
  and
  I hope it's alright with you

  Evelyn

  darling.

NINETEEN
A MURDER SCENARIO

Sally
Honestly
We're waiting for her to die.

Just . . .

Visiting the ruins until

Set us free

Catapult us into the next . . .

Him on his own

More on his own

More   with . . . (*her*)

Shakes her head.

Anyway . . .
think about that *tomorrow*, Scarlett!

To Robin . . .

Go on . . .

Robin is thinking deeply . . .

Robin
It's set in a society where euthanasia is
punishable by *death* . . .

Sally
. . . Kind of death?

Robin
The worst kind.

Sally
Boredom.

Robin
Yeah . . . Dad's the main executioner . . . you
get strapped into a chair . . . he does his Golfing
Triumphs

Sally
or his Courtly Love in Medieval Literature . . .

Robin
until you . . . (*die*) . . . it doesn't *matter*
. . . the *mise en scène* is the *mother* has to be
murdered by the children . . .

Sally
. . . it's a bit fucking *Freudian* . . .

Robin
Archetypal. Mythic Dimensions . . .
to save their father
from . . . wearing himself out, dying and leaving
the children . . .

Sally
poor fucking *orphans* . . .

Robin
ex-*actly* . . . but the children have to commit the
perfect murder.

Sally
So they get away with it.

Robin
Clean away.

Sally
Okay.

They both think long and hard . . .

Sally
We can't go for the obvious . . .
the stealthy pillow over the sleeping face . . .?

Robin
Dull. Been done. Don't you think?

Sally agrees physically.
Evelyn wakes up . . . speaks to somewhere . . . not someone . . .

Evelyn
it's   colours
it's   with a lot of about
oh
where do you live
where are you
are   you?

Robin
Should be something *devilishly fiendishly* clever . . .

Sally
Who's our audience sympathy with?

Evelyn
There's a!!!
Isn't it . . .

She points to her ear . . . indistinct noise in it.

(*Very indignant.*) I think she might have *said* something!

Sally touches her mother gently, distracted . . .

Evelyn (*appears to be thinking very deeply . . .*)
I'm pretty sure it was a *Tuesday* . . .

Robin
Okay.

The very clever brother has a workshop like
Ryan O'Neal's in *The Driver* . . .
he's a firearms expert . . .
he's a perfectionist
he's an inventor . . .

Evelyn
No, no
my *brown* leather handbag!
Ttt!
Ttt!
Ttt!
(*Disbelieving contempt.*) . . . I mean . . . *really*!

Sally
What's the dull sister doing . . .?

Robin
She's looking after her mother . . . establishing a
caring façade . . . while the very clever brother
perfects . . . a bullet made of . . . *ice*!

Sally
Ice?

Evelyn (*laughing delight* . . .)
. . . one of them had just a dab of white fur here (*chest*)
like a little *cravat*!

Robin
And the caring sister comes in . . .
fires the ice bullet throught the mother's brain . . .
kills her . . .
then it *melts*!
The evidence is thus . . . destroyed!

Sally
Leaving only the dull sister at the scene of the crime . . .

with the *gun*!

Robin
Damn!

an ice *gun*?

Evelyn
Give me that
give me that . . .

Screws up an imaginary, tiny piece of paper.

Thank you!

Sally
Lose the gun.

Robin
Yes.

Sally
Lose he's a firearms expert . . .

Robin
Well . . .

Sally
Keep he's a perfectionist . . .
but make him a really wussy nerdy
anorak . . .

Robin
Oh . . .

Sally
Keep the ice. Keep the workshop. But he mends *clocks*.
Keep the caring sister façade. Nerdy brother makes an
ice *darning* needle. Caring sister brings it in in her
    lapel . . .
takes it out . . . (*Stabs.*) . . . through the . . . some hole
    here . . .
Done. Murder Weapon is disappeared by The Body

it has murdered.
No evidence.

Robin
Final shot. Designer gear . . . posh hotel terrace.
They've inherited.

Sally
No one suspects?

Robin
Oh, they *suspect* . . . but they can't
prove anything.

They rest. A job well done.

Evelyn
ttt! (*Disapproval.*)

ma . . . (*Explanatory.*)

sfa . . . (*Remembers.*)

ce   (*Yes, that was it.*)

ce   (*Yes, simple, that was it . . .*)

She sits very still . . . as . . .

Sally
So
a steady trudge
through ever thicker and thicker mud

*A Casablanca-style map with a white dash-line
moving across it, slower and slower . . .*

Robin (*his dramatic voice-over accent*)
across the mile upon mile
of bleak and featureless terrain . . .
the waiting
the prison

83

the dread terror of a no man's land
trying to obtain the exit veezays
to a state of complete indifference . . .

TWENTY
A STATE OF COMPLETE INDIFFERENCE

Peter sees Evelyn, Evelyn stands.
She is mewing with distress, rather like a kitten . . .

Peter
What is it?
Evelyn?
Darling?
What's wrong?

Evelyn
Mewww!

Sally
Mum?

She feels her mother, checks her out . . . physically . . .

She's wet herself.
Dad . . .

Peter goes for . . .

Robin . . . cloth . . . through there . . .

Robin goes for . . .

Did you have a little accident . . . ?

*Peter comes back with clothes, large incontinence
nappy . . . Robin with flannel, etc . . .*

Robin
Shouldn't we get someone . . . ?

Sally (*mock stern*)
We rellies are *encouraged* to
help . . .

Robin
Oh God.

Sees the incontinence pad.

Oh my God!

Sally
Quite. Brace yourself . . . she's not keen
on this . . .

*She isn't. Changing and washing Evelyn is quite a
team effort. Sally is adept, Peter less so, Robin
hopeless but willing and squeamish. Evelyn mews,
complains physically and vocally, wanders off when
possible. All together now . . . this is the 'fight
sequence' . . . The three of them start off serious,
but . . .*

Fuck!
Dad . . . she's heading off!
Stand still, Mum, stand . . .
No . . . hold her . . . she'll make a noise . . . but she's
just . . .
one leg . . .

Robin (*same time*)
Here!
Here!
Here!
Look . . . I'll hold . . .
look . . . I'll hold . . . no, look . . . I'll hold . . .
here . . . I've got it . . .
okay . . . I've got it . . .

okay . . . I've got it . . .

Peter (*same time*)
. . . She would hate this . . . Sally! . . .

hated being seen nude . . . Robin! . . . your mother . . .

such a degrading, Sal! . . . no, darling . . . Robi . . .

Sally, pass me . . .

Robin, get me that . . .

Halfway through, exhausted, they drop their guard.
Evelyn wanders off . . .

Rolly! . . . Sabin! . . . she's off again . . .

They start laughing . . . reluctantly . . . then in the
next stage . . . a lot . . . until, by the end . . . all three
are laughing . . .

Robin (*all old jokes*)
I'll head her off at the pass, Kimo Sabe . . .!

Peter
No . . . you stay here, I'll surround her!

Sally
It is a far, far better thing we do now,
than we have ever done!

Following speeches at once . . . Evelyn is enjoying
herself. Laughing delightedly . . .

Sally
Now . . . just need to hold her steady while we . . .
now . . . weather eye out weather eye out for . . . *see*!
now . . . steady as she blows steady as she . . .
now . . . now stop . . . now . . . it's not funny . . .
now stop! Janet Reger! . . .
now . . . she needs to *step* into . . .
now . . . now . . .
Now!

Peter

Look what I've brought you, darling?
A present!
Look . . . lovely!
Lingerie!
Beautiful!
Janet Reger!
Gorgeous!

Robin

Okay. On the case. Up to speed now.

Up to speed.
Roll cameras
. . . *and* action! . . . it's okay . . . we can cut it . . .
we can tighten it up . . .
I've got it! Okay! I've got it!

The task is completed. Their wife/mother is changed and dry. Evelyn wears the kingfisher blue dress, no shoes. All four sit exhausted in a row of chairs . . . all four panting, smiling.

As their breathing returns to normal, Evelyn gets the hiccups. This makes them all laugh again. Peter fetches water for his wife. She won't drink.

They stop smiling. Evelyn falls asleep. The others watch her. Peter pats her hand, her head . . . and goes.

Sally brings forward the dark navy court shoes, not the black, fits them on her mother's feet as . . .

Sally

I suppose at the end of the day . . . Jimmy . . .
A wedding's about . . .
some notion of
unconditionality . . .

TWENTY-ONE
UNCONDITIONAL LOVE

Grace appears. Flowers and a whoopee cushion.

Grace
Thought I'd make the first move.
Be consistent.

Flowers.

For your mother.

Whoopee cushion.

For you.
Thought you could do with a laugh . . .

Sally
My mother's actually not . . .
she's
in a state of complete indifference.

Grace
Is she?
Are you?
. . . you look like the robber's dog . . .

Sally
Thank you.
Your colloquial English is really coming on . . .

Grace
Thank you.

Sally
Might as well give it a go . . .

Not talking about the book idea but . . .

Something fucking *concrete*!

TWENTY-TWO
MEETING THE FAMILY

Into . . .

Sally
Dad . . . this is Grace.

My brother Robin.

As Grace, Robin and Peter stickily shake hands, greet:

and this is the relative formerly known as
'Mum'.

Grace
Hello, Doctor Swan.

Sally
This is Grace.

Evelyn is quite inert.
    Grace gives Evelyn the flowers. No response.

Sally
Barely eating now
barely   there

Robin
you know in the first beat Rick and Elsa
are in love . . . and the whole story is gonna be
about Love versus Duty . . .

Bergman is always starlit
Bogart too.
They're special.
Their Love is . . .
They are apart . . . but somehow . . .
the light connects them . . .

Evelyn remains inert.
  Sally . . . the whoopee cushion . . .

Sally (*brings out the whoopee cushion . . .*)
Do you remember this?
Evelyn?
Mum?

  Sally blows up the whoopee cushion. Demonstrates it.
  Evelyn looks at Grace.

Evelyn
Beautiful!

  She is alight with love.
  Sally sings 'The Look of Love'.
  Robin and Peter throw confetti.

TWENTY-THREE
A PHOTOGRAPHIC MEMORY

All five are in separate spaces. Fog starts to roll in about
them . . . Each is lit . . .

Sally
A wedding story.

  She is holding the hat she described earlier . . .

Grace
I got married.
I got married.
I got married.

Sally
I was finally true to my gene pool . . .

Peter
I didn't go into details at the Golf Club.

Just said, 'I'm taking Evelyn to see Sally.
She's having a bit of a party.'
I say 'She's a Career Girl!'
Both my children are . . . it's their Careers
that are most important to them.
Grace. *Lovely* Girl.
But . . .
and this business about them having *children* . . .

It's too horrendous to think about now . . .

Grace
I found this *Humanist* minister to bless the union.

Sally
Danish! (Of course!)

Peter (*shaking his head throughout this . . .*)
Woman minister!
Humanist!
Purple sort of outfit.
Very nice speaking voice, though
Very clear in all the . . . / confusion

Sally
It really has a happy ending, this story.
Don't kid yourself.
Weddings are *always* about Family!
My mum *did* come to my wedding.
I *did* get married.
A small affair
bizarre
odd
unreligious.

Peter
Some of the *people* . . .

Sally
Unblessed
two women . . .
she'd have *hated* it . . .
Half way through the best woman's speech . . .

Peter
Dear me!

Robin
Mum farted.

Sally
Great big wet loud fart.

Grace
Everyone paused . . .

Sally
What to do? Pretend nothing had happened.
Concorde had just flown over?
Mum decided for us.

Robin
Mum . . . smiled.

Sally
Actually . . . it wasn't just a fart . . .
it was actually a very big, satisfying shit.
My mum's never been good with cream.

Peter
Darling!
Evelyn!
Darling!

Sally is grinning, Peter is grinning . . . as the light fades on her . . .

Robin
We're in the hangar

it's a cold night
chilly for Casablanca . . .
an old plane . . .
it doesn't look like it can *taxi*
let alone *fly* . . .

Sally (*disapproving*)
This metaphor . . .!!!

Robin
Fog
Fog everywhere . . .
the last scene at the airport is where they all *escape*
and the Good go off to fight Bad . . .

whether
on foot
by auto . . .
or plane . . .
everyone finally gets some sort of
exit-veezays . . .
it's where everyone *flies* . . .

The light fades slowly.

The End.

FROZEN

Acknowledgements

The author wishes to express her gratitude to Marian Partingon for her words and her courage.

Marian Partingon's article, 'Salvaging the Sacred: Lucy, My Sister', was first published in *Guardian Weekend*, 18 May 1996, and subsequently in *The Guardian Year '96* (Fourth Estate, 1996, ISBN 1–85702–551–2; now published by Quaker Books, ISBN 0–85245–353–1).

The author also wishes to acknowledge the inspiration of Dorothy Otnow Lewis, MD, and her work with Dr Jonathan Pincus concerning the neuropsychiatric characteristics of murderers, as profiled in Malcolm Galdwell's article 'Damaged', published in the *New Yorker* of 24 February 1997. Anyone wishing to read further about the subject should see Dr Lewis's book, *Guilty by Reason of Insanity* (Ballantine, 1998). Anyone withing to learn more about the psychology explored in this play should go to www.gladwell.com.

Frozen was first performed at the Birmingham Repertory Theatre on 1 May 1998, with the following cast:

Nancy Anita Dobson
Ralph Tom Georgeson
Agnetha Josie Lawrence
Daughter Gloria Nicholls
Guard Matthew Seymour
Voice of David Nabkus Joel Kaplan

Directed by Bill Alexander
Designed by Ruari Murchison
Lighting by Tim Mitchell
Music by Jonathan Goldstein

This production was revived in the Cottesloe Theatre auditorium of the National Theatre, London, on 28 June 2002.

The play received its New York premiere at the MCC Theatre on 25 February 2004, and this production transferred to the Circle in the Square Theatre on Broadway on 4 May 2004.

Characters

Ralph
Nancy
Agnetha
Voice of David
Guard

Act One

ONE
FAREWELL TO NEW YORK

New York street sounds . . . busy, whirling traffic and voices. Stops abruptly as light reveals . . . Agnetha, hallway of her apartment, New York. Checking her airline tickets, passport.

Agnetha
Yes.
yes.
yes.
yup.
yeah.
yo.

All is ready. She looks around. Looks through a doorway.

Bye room.

Gives the room a little wave.

Bye bedroom.
bathroom.
office.

She salaams gravely.

Bye home.

They all get waves, thumbs up, high-sings as appropriate. Until . . . she's ready. She picks up airline tickets, carry-on bag. She's ready. Then she unclenches her jaw . . . and her teeth start chattering.

Oh no.
I do not need this.
Not now.
Please.

But it is now. She puts down her tickets. Her teeth chatter uncontrollably. She succumbs loudly to the chattering . . .

er g-g-g-g-g-g-g-g
oo g-g-g-g-g-g-g
okay
out
good.

She waits again. Then tears fill her eyes and she starts blubbing. She encourages herself to cry . . . then bawl . . . there is something deliberate and good humoured about it . . . as if she is two people . . . one expressing emotion, the other encouraging it out . . .

mmmmuuuuuuurrr . . .
mmmmmmaaaaaaaaaaa . . .
yes, come on . . .
wwwwwaaaaaaahhhhhhh . . .
mmmmmmaaaaaaaaaahhh . . .
come on . . .
plane to catch . . .!
oh boy . . .

The bawling moves into keening and howling, so Agnetha must pick up her carry-on bag, which she screams into, muffling the sound somewhat. She screams and screams. Finally . . .

Okay.
finished?
Finito?

She checks.

yes.
yep.
okay.
good.

Picks up her travel documents, bag, etc. again.

yes yes yes yup yeah yo.

She calls loudly through the walls.

Sorry, Mrs Lipke!
The Big Noise is leaving!
Sorry, Mr Chen!
Crazy Horse is outta here!

She leaves for the airport. The sound of a large plane flying over . . . heading towards . . .

TWO
FAMILY LIFE

The gentle chirrup, hum, buzz of an English garden . . . Nancy, home, her back garden, evening, idly nipping buds off.

Nancy
    I should have gone round myself with those garden
        shears.
    Mother and I've never seen eye to eye on shrubbery.
    I'm prune-to-a-dormant bud
    but she'll be instigating a slash-and-burn-regime.
    She's let her Clematis Montana Alba do its own thing.
    I said 'they like their feet in the shade and their head
        in the sun' but she's plonked it
    in a south-facing bed

sandy soil

and it's gone on the rampage over into next door's
specialty alpines.

I offered to go round myself tomorrow and cut it back
for her

but she says 'It's Bridgnorth tomorrow'

Always leaves it to the last minute and then its got
to be

done This Minute Now Immediately.

So I asked for volunteers but that was like getting

someone to sign up for active service . . .

Bob's got Nautilus training . . .

and what's *that* all about . . . ?

A plane flies overhead. Nancy 'tuts' gently.

Been very happy with his flab till now

and I always say 'I'm very partial to your love
handles'

when we have a cuddle

but

well

so I need one of the girls to look lively

But Ingrid's 'Off' Grandma at the moment because of
The Make-Up Question

so I think easier all round if I send Rhona . . .

but Rhona's so good I always put on her

and I try to be fair

so I gird my loins to tackle Ingrid

in spite of it being like negotiating with Attila The Hun
these days . . .

I've taken a Deep Breath . . .

when suddenly Crash Bang Wallop

Holy War breaks out upstairs! . . .

'What Is It Now?' . . . I go – and that's when Bob
slithers out . . .

He's so . . . *sneaky* these days . . .

No 'Goodbye then Nancy love . . .'
well
In The War Zone . . .
There's a Max Factor Thick-Lash mascara wand
gone missing from Attila's *private* drawer
and who's Suspect Number One . . .?
Ingrid goes into Rhona's room
to obligingly fetch her for me,
drags her back by her *hair*, so I *separate* them
and look at Rhona.

She smiles.

She looks like a panda!
Great black-rimmed eyes.
I say to Ingrid 'go on, give her a bamboo shoot'
wrong thing to say . . .
'Mum! Rhona's not *funny*!
You should take this *seriously*.'
I say 'Who takes *me* seriously about a ceasefire on
this Fighting?'
and I pop in 'So . . . Ingrid . . . why don't you go
    round to
Grandma's for a bit of peace?'
and she's almost hooked when I add . . . 'And you
    could take
the garden shears while you're at it . . .'
and she's off again 'I'm just an unpaid scivvy in this
establishment . . . I wish I was an orphan . . . I wish
    somebody
would adopt me . . . nobody loves me . . .
everybody loves Rhona best . . .'
I say hopefully 'Now stop that nonsense . . .
I love you both equally in different ways.'
I don't.
I don't love either of them *at all* at the moment!
Or Bob!

Or Mother!
Any of them!
They can all go to hell for all I care.

Quite close by, a van accelerates . . .

But anyway
somehow it happens
Ingrid has me agreeing to let her go out
and chain of command's put the youngest soldier on
    secateur duty!
Little Panda.
My mother's going to think I'm letting *her* wear
make-up too young and be Reading The Riot Act! . . .
That's why Rhona's not back yet.
Yes!!!

THREE
A BAD PATCH

Ralph, in his room, washing his hands at a sink.

Ralph
You know
it's one of those days
you're just going to do it
you might do it
I suppose mostly I'm a bit of a cold fish

He dries his hands carefully on a small, clean towel.

but then, these times
things hot up
It's been a bit of a bad patch for me . . .
fucking landlady . . .
pardon my French . . .
despite I told her I don't eat lamb

despite I told her I'm not a big eater . . .
despite I made that clear . . .
turns up on the plate
and I've eaten it before I've said
'This isn't lamb is it . . .?'
and it *was* . . .

*Takes a small bottle of hand lotion, pours a dollop on
one palm, starts to rub it into both hands.*

and I've gone out with
hoojit . . . Raymond Quantock . . .
and that wassname from work . . . Dick Bottle . . .
and I've kept up with them putting it away . . .
otherwise . . .
and drunk five lagers
and two . . .

Counts in his head.

. . . four . . .
Jack Daniels
and I've gone over on that damn foot again . . .
lightning strike of pain . . .
and it's put me in a strop
nobody better mess me with
nobody better
been like . . . offish
and . . .

He's on a street somewhere.

I just see her
and decide
I'm going to get her in the van
I just want to keep her for a bit
Spend some time with her.
I just do it.
It's a rush of blood.

Hello.
Hello.
I said 'Hello'
are you deaf?
It's rude to ignore people.
Are you loony?
You're loony.
I'm only being polite.
No need to get the hump.
Not with me.
I just said 'Hello.'
Hello.
Hello.
Hello.
I'm saying 'hello' to you.
Least you can do is make conversation.
Kind of world is this
folk can't be sociable?
Polite.
Least you can do is make a response.
It's Bad Manners if you don't.
Bad manners.
Rude.
I said 'Hello'
Hello
Hello
Hello
Hello
Hello then . . .
finally . . .
finally . . .
she goes
'Hello'.

I think she quite liked me

oh yes

She was interested.

The van's down here
it's only fifty yards away
it's convenient
obviously
the back door's not locked
because I've thought ahead
obviously
she wants to come.

I've got cushions in the back
And a sleeping bag.
Obviously.

sometimes you're fucked by
circumstances
things don't go your way.

Picks something up. Regards it.

The garden shears
I don't bargain for
but
in the event
they turn out
useful
and add to it all
passing off
efficiently
but
logistically
she's persuaded it's time
to get in the van
you make it work
she's in the van.

Lovely evening
Sunny . . . but with a light southerly breeze . . .

FOUR
NATURE TABLE

Nancy, Rhona's bedroom, seven months later . . . a window overlooking the garden.

Nancy
This is Leo.

A small, threadbare soft-toy lion. She smiles slightly.

He's bald where she played Hairdressers on him.
'Rhona's Rough Cuts'.

Ingrid's making me a cup of coffee.
She's like the Catering Corps these past few days.
Mum, do you want a cup of hot chocolate?
Mum, shall we have a milky drink?
Mum, Cherry Bakewell?

I've lost nearly two stone.
I've gone back to smoking.
Cast Iron Excuse.
Even my mother has to let me.

It's bad today because it's Rhona's
birthday tomorrow and they say
Missing Children often phone on their
birthdays
get in touch . . .

She holds her stomach. Swallows.

so I thought
clean her room
her Nature Table's a bit dusty

give me something to do

when she comes back

everything will be nice
everything be the same
everything familiar.

That's gorse
with some sheep's wool tangled in it
From Brecon Beacons.
I got stuck between a lamb and its mother
the mother *ran* at me . . .
I ran like billy-o
the girls fell over laughing!
Rhona found this in the gap . . .
we had cheese and chutney sandwiches.

A cold wind blows . . .

Brecon Beacons.
She loved that day!
Wales! She's maybe . . .

Thinks.

No. We leafletted Wales.

This is her witch stone
it's a witch stone if it has a
natural hole in it.
See.

Looks through it.

You can see things in a witchy way . . .
it's magic.

Holds it tightly in her hand, eyes tight closed. Making a wish.

Kept it there

mmm.

Puts it back exactly.

What are you doing on here, Leo?

You live on the bed!

Somebody's been in here . . .
maybe Bob . . .
to primp and preen in private!
I know what's going on and
I know who with.
It's all gone a bit softly-softly and undercover
what with The Disappearance . . .
but if it's over I'm Raquel Welch!

I don't care !

These books are different.

Ingrid!

It is stifling her . . .

Washing up
Cleaning
Doing
Helping!
Well it's not!
I don't want anyone in here moving her things
round I want to keep it exactly as it was!
If I have to get Bob to put a lock on that door
I will!

Rhona

where are you?

I know you're somewhere!

FIVE
MOVING ON

Ralph brings a suitcase into his room.

Ralph
That incident up Scotland
not down to me
I operate in a southwards direction
Midlands Leicester Home Counties

Not fucking Scotland
Not cold icy windy Scotland!
Anybody with a *brain* would know that's Too Far!
Too far from my centre of operations.
I mean you're looking at transportation
something what over two hundred miles . . .
Where's the sense in that?
Where's the efficiency?
You've got to keep things *clean* in every sense
I never touch *anything* outside an eighty-mile radius
of my centre of operations
oh no
oh no
once you've got a site sorted
well, you don't mess with *that*, do you?
obviously
but
mud sticks

I got 750 pounds for the van.
Him who bought it
didn't notice the chassis's all rust
fuck him if he can't make a thorough check!

I'll get something a later reg.
That's been a bit of an unlucky vehicle for me.

So's this place.
Landlady . . .
despite when the police come here
they found nothing
despite it's clean
despite I'm clear
despite that . . .
has gone 'sling your hook
don't want you here
go
clear off . . .'
and I've no comeback on it in law!
cunt
Fucking Cheek! . . . 'scuse me!
Kept it like a New Pin!

Who do they think they are?

Should be a law
You should have a guarantee of security
for your money.

Good job I done planning here.
Good job I thought logistically . . .
had these in lock-up.

Taps head.

You've got to wake up very early to get ahead of me!
Oh yes
Oh yes!

Videos are packed, titles mostly upright. He turns one round. Takes out a notebook. Refers to it.

Lollitots
Lesbian Lolita
Little Red Riding Hood

*Beautiful, romantic, yearning music . . . sounds of
summer countryside.*

Little Ones In Love
Child Love
Lesbian Lolita at School

*He turns a video the right way round . . . mock
exasperation . . . he loves these videos.*

Lolita's Examination
Lolita's Auntie
Pre-Teen Trio

Sweet Patti
Sweet Susan
Little Linda
Baby Bonnie . . .

These cost!
What!!
So I put them in safe storage
obviously.
Protect my investment.
I've had to get these from abroad!
Amsterdam, some of these!
France.
Denmark.

Nobody's having these

they're precious
oh yes
oh yes

I'm going to have to safe-keep these in
my centre of operations
until I get a new residence
I'm going to have to get some sort of
protective filing system.

I'm not sure that shed's efficient
dampwise . . .

He makes a short list.

Now I'm moving on

new start

oh yes
oh yes.

A car drives off. Overhead steady thrum of plane as . . .

SIX
THIS FLIGHT TONIGHT

*Agnetha, on an aeroplane, laptop on her lap, keying
sporadically . . . also drinking from a plastic cup . . .*

Agnetha (*keys*)
'Serial Killing . . . a forgivable act?'

*She drains her drink. Presses the 'Flight Attendant'
summoning light . . . No response . . . Keys.*

'Judicial Revenge . . . a political choice?'

*Pours non-existent drops of liquid from two or three
small in-flight bottles of brandy into the glass. Presses
'Flight Attendant' call again . . . No response. Keys.*

Brandy Refill . . . a Forlorn Hope?
Yes . . . I think so . . . Close File . . . Save? . . .
Shit . . . Email . . . oh yes please . . .

She starts writing furiously . . .

Dear David,
Dearest Damn Fuck You Then David
I hate you

I hate hate hate hate hate you
All the people on this flight are in mortal danger and
it is your fault.
You will be responsible for these multiple deaths
as we plummet out of the sky
into the sea a very very very long way down there
right under where I am sitting.
on *big* air
over *big* sea
it is your fault
you and your Big News
you and your Hilarious Damn Bad Behaviour have
alchemised me into
Miss Fudge Feeling of Washington Square
who is shit-scared of flying!
Give me back my real brain!
Hand over my native intelligence!
When we crash
because of you
because of you taking away my faith in anything at
 all . . .
I take innocent people with me . . .
Lily-White Souls perish here . . .

She pours a non-existent drop of brandy into her glass.

Although the stewardess serving me deserves to die . . .
a lonely, painful, lingering, agonising death
for the impressive number of
times she has wilfully ignored my request for brandy
and for a certain radiant spitefulness over her
inability to provide me with a vegetarian meal . . .
I imagine pouncing,
sinking my teeth into her neck just above her
white pretty blouse and biting out her throat
murmuring all the time

'How's *this* for going with
The Meat Option?'

*She covers her laptop screen with a 'don't copy my
homework' arm, against her next-door neighbour.
Looks out of the window.*

Still over sea.

Watery death for us all then . . .
Lovely, violent in-flight movie.
Many good and worthless men perished
in explosions of bright red blood.

I thought of you.

Her eyes fill. She wipes them surreptitiously . . . then:

You bastard
you make me frightened of everything!

*The plane flies on. Ping of 'Fasten Seat Belts' sign
flashing on . . .*

Oh   my   God   !

Reads computer.

SEND?
Why not?

The plane flies on.

SEVEN
FLAME

Nancy, smart suit, drink, her house, four years later.

Agnetha
It always works . . .
but it was magnificent tonight!

I get whoever's in charge of introducing
to say quite simply . . .
'From the organisation *FLAME* . . .'
Mrs Nancy Shirley . . .
and I find if you just give it a minute
. . . they settle . . .
and then I go . . .

She is in a school hall, many silent people.

Ladies and gentlemen of the . . .
and I fill in where we are . . .
Tonight it was a Parent/Teachers thing
in Spalding . . .
Ladies and gentlemen of the *whatever* . . .
on April 17th, 1980,
my daughter,
Rhona . . .

and I pick up her photograph . . .
walked out of my house
to go to her grandma's house
she never got there
she never came back
she was ten.
She's been missing for
five years.
She will be fifteen years old tonight.
I know she's alive.
I have Faith.
Every night I pray
that whatever reason is stopping her coming home
will be removed
and that she'll phone
or write
or just knock on the door
and say 'Mum, it's me.'

Bob says he always watches that bit
it gives him a chill down his back he says
I've got him giving me lifts to these dos
it's brought us closer together,
cemented us
stopped that nonsense
with that Nautilus trainer woman.
I've got him on jogging . . .
He said 'when you showed our Rhona's
photograph tonight, I thought, we're going
to get lucky this time . . .'

and then I pick up the *other* photograph
and go . . .

This . . .
is Robert Greaves.
He disappeared on his way to
Boy Scouts on September 14th, 1976.
He was fourteen.
Today's his birthday . . .

You could have heard a *pin* drop . . .

He's twenty-three . . .
And four weeks ago he walked through
his parents' front door in Braintree, Essex,
and said 'Mum, I'm back'
because we at *FLAME* found him!
Even though my little girl
my Rhona is still out there
I *rejoice* for Mr and Mrs Greaves
that our organisation
was able to reunite them
with their Robert . . .

And Bob has the leaflets ready . . .
because *FLAME* is about

just that . . .
keeping that flame of hope alive
keeping it burning
so that our missing children
can see its light
and feel its warmth
and come towards it!

It's funny
I feel I was born to do this
I found nothing so easy to do as this
it's funny
but this is when I feel most alive . . .

Returns to her room.

So . . .
I'm not best pleased to get back to a
drunk Ingrid
ashtray piled
another fag burn on the settee arm . . .
She says
'I had a bad dream
I'm in the frozen frozen Arctic
I've lost somebody
the body's under the ice
but it's getting harder and colder
the ice is building up . . .'
I say 'No wonder, you've let the thermostat
go off . . .'
but she *wails* like a great soft thing . . .
says . . .

'I look for a hole
I look for a seal hole
but there's no hole
the body's down there
but it's all getting whiter.'

Pause.

I say 'Well never mind do you want some
drinking chocolate?'
but she's off again.
'But do you know what I do then?'

And I say no what
and she laughs

daft mad laugh
and says
'Oh
I go inside of course
to get warm.'

Pause.

Bloody girl!

Bloody girl!

*A confused explosion of time-markers . . . New Year
bells . . . bonfire fireworks . . . Christmas . . . time
passing . . . clocks.*

EIGHT
TATTOO YOU

*Ralph, summer shirt, bench. He has tears in his eyes.
Twenty years later.*

Ralph
Oya
Oya
Oya

Limping . . . sits down, rubbing his ankle.

Fuck . . . this fucking hurts!
Stinging!
Oya!
But you got to suffer for something worthwhile!

Oh yes
Oh yes.

*Pulls up his trouser leg, down his sock . . . reveals a
fresh tattoo.*

This is 'The Grim Reaper'
seventy-five quid
three hours twenty-three minutes
two needles
five colours!
it's a traditional design
big with bikers
you get sickle *and* scythe.
Brilliant.

'The Needlemaster' in Burley.
good service.
Cup of tea if you want
and clean
spanking clean.

Not like

(*Contempt.*) 'Body Art Tattooing, Dersingham'!

Shows a tattoo on his right arm.

Sunburst Dagger of Death.
Got done December for Christmas . . .
Needler's a fucking woman . . .
'Gazza's booked. I'm registered.
Take it or leave it . . .'

Suppressed rage.

Well, I couldn't come back
obviously . . .
so . . .
she's jabbing and poking . . .
one hour forty-three minutes . . .
came up like a balloon!
Cunt!

Tattoo on forearm . . .

Compared to
This.

Can't remember.

This.

Aw. Shit . . .

Strokes tattoo.

Madonna and Child
four colours . . .

Herculean struggle to remember . . .

'Tattoo Shack'!
'The Tattoo Shack'!

Bridgnorth. A456.
Ex-biker
three hours forty . . .
fucking craftsman!

Other arm, forearm . . .

'Chuck's Custom Tattoos'.
I'm not happy with that.
Too plain.
I'm going to get it adorned

Upper arm . . .

as this.
I designed that.
That's an original.
Angels fighting devils.
With leafy-tree background.

Quoting.

'Your design or mine.
Call now or just pop in.
Thousands of designs to choose from
Professional and friendly.' A4112.
'Sacred Art' . . . Leominster, this one.

Good.

Rubs his newly-tattooed ankle again.

Oya.
Oya.
Oya.

I'm going to have to take my mind
off this

He stands up, flexing his foot.

Oh yes
oh yes
don't wanna be feeling this all the way back

Somebody to talk to
spend a bit of time with
would be ideal
obviously
sun's hot

Sees something . . . becomes very still, focused.

Hello.
I said 'Hello'.

Hello.
Hello.
Hello.

A young girl laughs somewhere . . .

NINE
CHICKENS COMING HOME

Nancy walking . . . three or four days later.

Nancy
Sun's so hot.

Four days ago
phone call from the police
they think they have some news for us
can they come over?

Terrible terrible restlessness anxiety
then two young policemen . . . *lads* . . .
one with fine soft hair like a kiddie's . . .
other lovely polished shoes
pitch up
say . . .
'We have apprehended a man in the
unsuccessful attempted abduction of a young girl . . .
subsequent inquiries have uncovered a lock-up shed
the earth floor contains the remains of other children
the man is now giving us names
one of them
he says
is   Rhona.'

*Sound of great ice floes breaking up, cracking,
churning . . .*

FROZEN

I wanted to go out for a walk
up a hill somewhere

find some fresh air
there's no air.

Message
after message
after message
on the ansaphone.
Newspapers
we must we must we must
want to talk to them.

Ingrid
comes over
makes something with noodles
can't touch it
but I show willing
twirl it around on the plate a bit with a fork.
Ingrid says
'Try with chopsticks . . . I'll show you how to . . .'
but I leave it all sitting there
dumped on the plate

puts me in mind of worms

I've given Bob some more paracetamol
his headache's approaching Gale Force . . .

All this time
I've been growing her up
she's been
he's had her buried away . . .

I wish this weather would break.

I wish it would pour it down.
It's unbearable.

Great Big Storm.

A huge storm breaks . . .

TEN
SWEATING

Ralph, a cell.

Ralph (*hand between his legs*)
Piss!
Shit!

They've just come the questions
all the time
all the . . . relentless
without thinking you might need a break
bit of time to think collect your thoughts . . .
so
obviously
when this fucking woman policeman cunt
comes the nice the interested the . . .
'Those are interesting tattoos,
did you get them all done in the same place?'
I'm not thinking I'm not sharp enough
logistically to understand
that they're putting me in the frame in
the picture in the *area* for
the incidents!

Sunburst Dagger of Death
logged
date
area
fucking woman needler
places me in the area where the
dark-haired little . . .

Same
Tattoo Shack, Bridgnorth
kid in the shorts . . .
I was there
Madonna and Child.

Really, statistically,
once they put that information
with my petrol book and receipts
and the real slip-up in terms of
efficiency over this latest incident . . .
I've got to let them take me on it!

So I admit
I give them my shed
centre of my operations
they get my special videos.

I'm helpful
polite
so
how come then
they're taking turns with the whispering and threats . . .
You're not a man.
That's not a man.
You're going to have to have ears in your neck boy
in your shoulders in your arse
every second in here
when you eat
think what we've put in there
think about it
and think about bum and knob and what
comes out of there boy . . . smegma come wank-juice
. . . I mean, the language . . .
and even when you're locked up alone don't sleep
boy because all around you we're lying eyes
wide open thinking what next what idea next

for you losing your eye say getting your knob
sliced like a breakfast sausage
somebody shoving somming like this . . .
up your smelly arse till you shit blood
snot in your food
don't ever rest don't ever sleep
yes, you keep your head down, boy
you keep flicking those eyes about
till we get you!

Not on!
oh no
oh no

ELEVEN
NEAR

Nancy, by a window, looking out.

Nancy
   Police
   the fair tufty-haired one said . . .
   there's something you should know . . .
   something he's said . . .
   where he took her . . .

   that shed on Far Forest Lane.
   He took her there
   all the time we were first looking
   she was just over there.

   I went past it!
   How many times?

   Not on her way to my mother's at all
   there
   if I'd thought   earlier

got up from *gardening* earlier
gone down there
spotted a light
heard a   oh   sound
seen across there
something that made me go across
investigate

she must have known how near I was
if she'd   made a noise
I could have heard her I think
oh

oh
oh.

A sound of clapping . . .

TWELVE
LOVELY TO BE HERE

Agnetha, a large, academic hall somewhere.

Agnetha
Oh
oh
oh
Well thank you!
What a warm reception!
Thank you!
I'm very touched. Sincerely.
It's terrific to be here!
England. I'm honoured.
London. I'm touched.
Ladies and gentlemen . . .
Please. Now . . .

Let me repay you for your very generous Visiting
Fellowship by . . .
So . . .
Let's see me earn my bucks!

*She gets businesslike. Takes up a place behind a
lectern. Notes. A screen backs up what she is saying.*

The title of my thesis is
'Serial Killing . . . A Forgivable Act?'
and it is a critical examination of the differences
between crimes of evil
and crimes of illness.
I will base my critique upon
A psychiatric and neurological study of
the criminal brain conducted by myself and colleagues
during my tenure as
Amex-Suntori Chair of Psychiatry
New York University School of Medecine . . .

Okay
the personal stuff . . .
My name is Dr Agnetha Gottmundsdottir . . .
My ancestors came to America
from a small frozen very cold ice-bound
place which experiences for a lot of the time
perpetual night . . .
so I guess it is in my Icelandic genes to want to take
myself and you, in my thesis . . .
to explore just such a frozen place . . .
But I am a *psychiatric* explorer.
So my chosen expedition will be . . .
The Arctic frozen sea that is . . .
the criminal brain.

Ralph's head lit as if it is an exhibit.

Let us take a look.

She walks over to stand behind Ralph, demonstrating
around his head, but not touching. A Prison Guard
stands some way off, watching.

The cortex is the thick covering of grey
matter on the upper part of every
human brain
and the function of the cortex
and, in particular,
those parts of the cortex
beneath the forehead known as
the frontal lobes
is to modulate the impulses that surge up
from within the brain.
The cortex and the frontal lobes
are there to provide judgement,
to organise behaviour
and decision-making
to learn and stick to
rules of everyday life.
Ladies and gentlemen . . .
they are responsible for making us human.

I intend here to examine
what goes wrong with that humanity . . .
which can make certain individuals appear inhuman
using data collected from case studies
conducted by myself and colleagues
of men who have received the death sentence over
the past ten years for their crimes in the US
plus my present casework here in England . . .
where of course you have abolished the death penalty.

Ralph Ian Wantage
is currently in Long Larton Maximum Security Prison
serving a life sentence without remission
for the abduction, sexual assault

and murder of seven young girls
over a period of twenty-one years . . .

*The light on Ralph extends. Agnetha and Ralph are in
the same space.*

Ralph
Cunt.

Agnetha
Doctor.
Let us be polite with one another, mm?

Ralph
I can be polite.
I've got manners.
I'm a gentleman.
Oh yes.
Oh yes.

Agnetha
Yes.
Good.

*Ralph assents . . . big accommodating gesture. As she
measures his head, he sniffs her. She writes.*

Ralph
Cunt.

Agnetha
No.
Chanel Number 19
and a mild and gentle soap.
Stop being dangerous, Ralph.

Ralph
If you know my name,
you know my reputation.

Agnetha
Sure I do.
Can you hold your hands apart
like . . .
and spread your fingers . . .
Good . . .

He copies her.

Interesting tattoo.

Ralph
Oh no, clever cunt.
What you after?

Agnetha
I'm looking for discontinuous,
jerky little movements . . .

As his fingers, arms jerk . . .

Ah-ah.

She holds up a finger, forty-five degrees to his left.

Would you let your eyes
follow my finger, please . . .?

His eyes follow jerkily.

Ralph
Oh . . .! Shite.

She stops.

Agnetha
Can we try that again . . .
can you try to watch it go smoothly across . . .?

Tries it again. Jerky again.

Ralph
Shite.

Agnetha
Okay. Good.
Now look at the ceiling
just with your eyes . . .

He cannot.

Ralph
Shite.
This has got to stop!

Agnetha
I'm sorry.
Just . . .
please stay still . . .

To Guard.

It's okay . . .
I'm just going to . . .

*She goes behind him, reaches over the top of his head.
He starts.*

Ralph
Hey, no way!

Agnetha
. . . touch him . . .
I'm sorry, I did not mean to startle you!
I'm not gonna harm you.
I'm gonna tap you on the nose . . .
Just let me . . .

*She taps a rhythm on the bridge of his nose. He blinks
rapidly, gets distressed as . . .*

Ralph
> Hey
> hey
> hey
> hey . . .

*Sound of girl laughing . . . Lights down on Ralph as
Agnetha moves away . . . showing us on her own
nose.*

Agnetha
> When you tap someone on the
> bridge of the nose, it's reasonable
> for the person to blink a coupla times
> because there is a threat from outside.
> When it's clear there is no threat . . .
> a person should be able to accommodate that.
> But if the subject blinks more than three times,
> that's what we call 'insufficiency of suppression'
> which may show frontal lobe disfunction.
> The inability to accommodate
> means you can't adapt to a new situation.

> There's a certain rigidity there.

> Like the person is icebound.

THIRTEEN
SUFFER

Nancy smoking, her house.

Nancy
> I'd like to see him die.
> Watch him
> suffer
> he wouldn't suffer like she suffered

but it would be something.
An eye for an eye
tooth for a tooth.
I want to see that.

Everybody at *FLAME*'s
been very understanding
the committee were in absolute agreement
when I suggested we shifted focus
from missing persons . . .
to spotlight an even more crucial area of
community responsibility . . .
Paedophile Identification . . .
Marjorie Alexander pressed my arm
and said 'we're with you two hundred per cent'
when I get up now
and say

'If we had known
ladies and gentlemen
that within a few hundred yards of us
in a rented lock-up shed
there was a known convicted paedophile . . .
we would have been vigilant
we would have been forewarned
we would have been able to protect our little girl . . .'
the clapping is always tumultuous,
people always stand up,
a few at first
then it's a full-blown ovation . . .
We're tapping into something very, very deep here

I got back tonight
somebody from an affiliated organisation's
sent me a video.
America
they've got a scheme

you can go and be there when they die
murderers
you get a run-up visit
they show you the electric chair
how it all works
they take you through the procedure.
The warders were *very* sympathetic . . .
the enforcement workers always are . . .
and then, you can be present,
members of victims' families
at that final moment.
He doesn't suffer like she suffered
but it would be something.

A sound of lightning connecting with earth source . . .

There was a *grandmother* on the video . . .
eighty-something, she went . . .
little grandkiddy shot stone-dead by a killer . . .
talk about guts!
She goes

Bad American accent.

'I kin fergive,
but I kain't fergit.'

English.

I can forgive,
but I can't forget.
Mother says . . .
'I'm a forgiving woman
but I can't forgive what he's done.
I'd be there, Nancy, I'd be there . . .'

Bob says, 'I'd be there.'
I said, 'If you were there, you'd go for him.'
He says 'I would . . . if there were a window of

opportunity, I'd be through it . . .'
He would.

Pause.

All through this, not a peep out of Ingrid.
Eating from a big economy bag of crisps.
Size of her since she gave up her smoking
and drinking!
Hasn't thought to hand them round.
Just . . . hugs the bloody bag to herself . . .
chomping . . .
Suddenly . . . she says
'I'm going off.
Travelling.
I thought India, Nepal.
The East.'

Why?

Why?
Danger
Hot
Filth
Dirt
I don't care.

FOURTEEN
FOUR FARM FUCK

Agnetha, with Ralph, prison. Guard on duty.

Agnetha
Okay. Good.
Give me as many words as you can
that begin with . . .
F.

Ralph
Four
fourteen
forty-four.

Pause.

farm.
farm.
farming.
farming.
farm.
farm.

Pause.

fuck.
fucker.
fucking.

He is pleased with these.

fuck.

Agnetha
Any more, Ralph?

Ralph
Four.
fourteen.
forty-four.

Pause.

four.

Agnetha
You've said that, Ralph . . .

Ralph
I'm not fucking stupid!
I'm not fucking stupid you know . . .

Agnetha (*pats his arm*)
Shhh.
It's all right.
It's not an intelligence test.
You do very well in intelligence tests.
You're not stupid.

As she walks away from him:

. . . you're manipulative and intense and
kinda mesmerising like *a rattlesnake* and you're a
   multiple
killer and I'd just really like a cigarette suddenly
but you're not . . .

Into lecture hall . . .

This is not an intelligence test.
If I asked Ralph to list . . . say . . . sixteen products
he might buy in a supermarket . . .
he would do just as well as anyone else . . .

Ralph
Beans, lamb chops, pizza, potatoes, Smash,
biscuits, lager, whisky, apples, carrots,
crab sticks, steak . . . hamburgers . . . Pop Tarts

Etc. and on . . . as . . .

Agnetha
That is a structured test,
with familiar objects.
The word-fluency test I have done asks
the testee to cope with situations
where there are no rules,
where they have to improvise,
where they make unfamiliar associations.
My colleague David Nabkus and I have
been conducting these tests for over twenty years . . .

Pause.

Sorry
something in my eye
sorry.

Ralph
economy sausages
fish fingers
frozen peas

Agnetha
and
normal is fourteen, give or take . . .
Anyone who does less than nine . . .
is abnormal.
And falls within mine and David Nabkus' study.

We believe Ralph is abnormal
and we believe we can show you
the reason why . . .

for what it's worth

hey David?

FIFTEEN
ABSOLUTELY NOTHING

Sound of machinery . . .

Nancy
Workman plaid shirt
came and knocked
said
'Mrs Shirley . . . we're going to have it down for you
that shed
do you want to come and watch?'

I said
'I do.'

We walked
it's no distance
and . . .

Nearer machinery . . . engines . . .

big mechanical digger . . .
. . . big heavy ball . . . he climbs in
he says 'where shall I start?'
I said
'that front bit where it happened'
and he hit it with the first swing

A heavy crunch, metal against stone . . .

and the corner of the shed caved in
and he went swinging at it again and again
and
within minutes
it was gone
it was like my heart torn out of my chest
and oh
there was nothing there any more
nothing at all
just nothingness

A sound of splintering ice floes . . .

oh
help
help
help

Rhona!

Ingrid!

SIXTEEN
THE BRAINS OF IT

Agnetha
At this stage,
Dr Nabkus, who is the neurologist in our
partnership,

Slight pause.

takes a detailed medical history.
In his absence

Slight pause.

. . . I will endeavour to find out
what he would find out . . .

*She sits. Ralph circles round her. She watches him for
a time.*

You have a little limp there, Ralph . . .

Ralph
No.

Agnetha
Yes, I think so.

*She watches him as he circles her . . . so he stands
still, behind her.*

Ralph.
Don't stand behind me.

Ralph
It frightens you.

Agnetha
No.
They stop us meeting if you . . .

Come in front of me.
Let me see this limp.

Ralph
No limp.

He walks to stand in front of her.

Agnetha
Mmmm.
Can you hop? On the right leg.
For just a little time?

Rolls his eyes because she is mad . . . but hops.

Good.
Now the left.

Ralph does so . . . staggers. Far away, something falls from a great height . . . fractures . . .

Ralph
Shite!

Tries again.

Shite!
Pardon my French.

Agnetha
Okay.
You're just proving something for me.
No Big Deal.
Come sit down.
Talk to me.

Ralph sits down. Agnetha regards him . . . then leans forward and goes to touch his forehead gently. Ralph flinches back, swatting her. She flinches back.

Ralph
Sorry!

Agnetha
  Sorry!

Ralph
  Sorry.

Agnetha
  Sorry.

Both look towards Guard. To Guard.

  Sorry.

To Ralph.

  I was just going to ask . . .
  how did you get that scar?

Ralph (*touches it*)
  This.
  Er.
  I fell off a roof
  blacked out
  bosh.
  I was pissed pissed
  and
  I was getting away from somebody
  and
  bosh
  just over and then whack
  nothing broken
  just like this bruise come up fucking large as an egg . . .

Agnetha
  How old were you?

Ralph
  'Bout . . . eighteen . . .
  probably . . . yeah . . . no no no! . . . this was a car!
  we got this car . . . and took it out for a burn yeah . . .

and whacked it into a wall yeah . . .
I wasn't driving
obviously
but I go smack! seat in front . . .

Agnetha
this was when you were . . .

Ralph
sixteen?
blood all in my eye

Right eye.

couldn't see fuck when we legged it!
but
hey . . .?
give us your hand . . .

Agnetha (*to Guard*)
I'm touching him, okay?
It's just investigative, okay?

Slowly she does . . .

Ralph
Feel there . . .

Agnetha
. . . oh yes . . .
what happened there?

Ralph
I fell down a mine shaft!
I was blacked out for hours yeah . . .
was running
didn't see it just didn't see it . . .
bosh
trip
bosh

    fall
    whack
    out!
    it was serious because it was same place as
    where my mam threw me in the sink . . .

Agnetha
    When was this?
    when your mom – mam threw you in the sink?

Ralph
    oh
    a kid
    little
    obviously . . .
    when she could get away with it still!

Agnetha
    Over the years
    Dr Nabkus and myself have studied
    more than 250 dangerous criminals . . .
    in significant numbers,
    these men have incurred physical damage to
    the brain.
    We have compiled a list of all the
    verifiable brain injuries suffered by
    fifteen randomly selected Death Row inmates . . .
    as you will see from the paper . . .
    page five, table D . . .
    the instances are many.

    After Dr Nabkus has finished
    his medical history . . .
    I look for evidence of child abuse . . .

    A sound of blustery wind . . .

SEVENTEEN
A LINE OF WASHING

Nancy, her kitchen garden, a pile of washing, a clothes line. March. Morning.

Nancy
Instead of letters
telling us where she was
how she was getting along and whatnot
these mucky little parcels start arriving
inside
cloth squares about this big . . .
bright colours
with foreign-type writing on . . .
Handkerchiefs?
Head squares?
Then a postcard . . .
'In Lhasa. Hope you got the Tibetan
prayer flags.
They are printed with spiritual blessings.
They are hung up each year
to signify
hope
transformation
and the spreading of compassion. As the year
progresses
the wind disperses the energy of the words,
which carry the power to pacify and heal
everything they touch.
Lots Of Love.

Ingrid.'

Shoved them in my bits and bobs drawer.
Daft business.

Then . . . the trial starts to happen . . .

She starts pegging out . . .

I say
can I have our Rhona's remains so we can at least
bury her . . .
letter comes back . . .
Ralph Wantage's solicitor insists on keeping the remains
as his 'exhibits' . . .
I carry the letter with me all day . . .
it's on the bedside table all night
I don't sleep
I think I am as near to being not alive any more
as I've ever been
I put the letter in my bits and bobs drawer
and there's those flag things

What she has pegged out are the Tibetan prayer flags.
A wind waves them.

it's a damn windy day
they flap and flap and
the gate opens and
this thin, thin, brown thing
says
'Hello, Mum, it's me.
See you got the flags then?
Cool.'

Ingrid.
Ingrid.
Ingrid.

EIGHTEEN
CONCLUDING MY ADDRESS

Agnetha, addressing her interested audience. Large, comfortable lecture hall.

Agnetha
Doctor Nabkus and I
observed a group of toddlers over three months . . .
half of whom had been subjected to
serious physical abuse
half of whom had not.
We were interested in how the toddlers
responded to a classmate in distress

Here is David's description of 'Martin'
an abused boy of thirty-two months . . .

She switches on the tape . . . sound of David Nabkus. We see Agnetha listening, watching . . .

. . . he tries to take the hand of the crying
other child, and when she resists, he slaps her
on the arm with his open hand . . .
He then turns away from her to look at the ground
and begins vocalising very strongly . . .
'Cut it out!
CUT IT OUT! . . .'
each time saying it a little faster and louder.
He pats her
but she becomes disturbed by his patting . . .
so he retreats,
he hisses at her
he bares his teeth . . .
then he begins patting her on the back again
his patting becomes beating
and he continues beating her

even though she's screaming . . .

Agnetha is with Ralph in the prison room. Tears are coursing down her cheeks, sobs interrupting her breathing. Ralph is watching her . . .

Sorry.

Ralph
Stop.

Agnetha
Sorry . . . it's just . . .

Ralph
Stop that.

Agnetha
I'm sorry.

A Guard, impassive, responds to Agnetha's signs that all is well. Ignores Ralph's agitation . . .

Ralph
Just stop it
okay
okay
just stop it.

Agnetha
I'm sorry.
It's just . . . this man . . . a good friend of mine . . .
a colleague . . .
has died recently . . .
I'm sorry.
Where were we?

Ralph
You put your chair very close in to the table.
You open your legs as wide as they'll go.
Then I put my hand slowly slowly

down so Chummy over there
sees nothing

Agnetha
Ralph . . .

Ralph
and I search with my fingers till they find
your pussy
your knickers are there . . .
so I go   rip!
my finger ends are touching pussy now.

Agnetha
Ralph . . .

Ralph
I find where you go in.
I position.
Then I ram in
obviously
again and again and again and again
oh yes
oh yes!

Agnetha
Guard . . .
You see
the second critical argument in my thesis
is that the mental abuse of children
causes profound and pathological changes in
the structure of the brain as surely as does physical
    injury
We brain-scanned the children
of severe neglect
We found that entire structures of their cortex
never properly developed . . .

these cortical regions were twenty to thirty per cent
   smaller
than normal . . .

Ralph (*to Guard*)
   What are you looking at?

Agnetha
   Abuse also disrupts the brain's stress-response system
   with profound results . . .
   when something traumatic happens . . .

Ralph (*to Guard*)
   What are you looking at?

Agnetha
   the brain responds by releasing
   several waves of hormones . . .
   the last of which is cortisol.

   Somewhere, some liquid starts dripping slowly . . .

   which is supposed to bring everything back to normal.
   The problem is . . . cortisol is toxic . . .

Ralph
   I'm sorry. Sorry.

Agnetha
   If someone is exposed to too much stress
   over too long a time . . .
   all that cortisol begins to eat away at the part
   of the brain known as the hippocampus
   which serves as the brain's archivist . . .
   organising and shaping memories,
   putting them in context
   placing them in space and time . . .

Ralph
   She was asking me something.

Agnetha

Abuse also affects the relationship between
the left hemisphere of the brain . . .
which plays a large role in logic and language
and the right hemisphere,
which is thought to play a disproportionately large
role in creativity and expression.

Ralph

She was *consulting* with me
obviously
oh yes
oh yes.

Agnetha

In the children we studied
not only was the abnormality twice as high
as a non-abused group,
but in every case
the abnormality was on the left
where *logic* dwells.

A sound of something breaking . . .

Ralph

It's a question of the doctor
doing research.

Agnetha

What you get is a kind of erraticness . . .
they can be very different in one situation
compared to another . . .
there is a sense that they don't have a
larger moral compass . . .

Ralph

She likes me!

Agnetha

In someone abused or neglected

the section of the brain involved
in attachment
in making emotional bonds
would actually look different
the wiring wouldn't be as dense,
as complex.

Ralph
She *wants* to spend time with me

Agnetha
They are literally lacking some brain organisation
that allows them to make strong connections
to other human beings . . .

Lights up once again on her and Ralph.

Ralph
Was I out of order then?

Agnetha
Yeah.
Sorta.
But it's okay, Ralph.
It's not your fault.
You can't help it.

NINETEEN
THE BONES OF IT

*Nancy, smart outfit, sits on something low, unsuitable,
lights cigarette with quivering hand.*

Nancy
Well.
Well.
Well.
. . . We've just come from the chapel of rest.

They still won't release her bones and . . .
I said 'I can't bear it, nothing's moving . . .'
and Ingrid says
in her new, quiet, calm . . . *round* . . . voice . . .
'let's take some stuff down then . . .
our stuff . . .
give her some   protection.'

Just been
just now

I thought they'd refuse
red tape
sub judice et cetera
but no . . .
Mortician showed us straight into the chapel of rest.
Her coffin.
Ingrid says 'We've got some things, we'd like to put
them with her . . .'
I thought he'd draw the line at that,
but no . . .
he takes a screwdriver out of his top pocket
unscrews the lid
takes it off and stands with it.
There's two cardboard boxes . . . different sizes . . .
DIY-archive system type . . . we've got them in the
     FLAME
office for files . . .
Ingrid points to the smaller one . . .
up the . . . up the head end . . .
and says 'Is this the skull?'
He nods.
'Go on' she says to me, very quiet, 'open it.'

It's

it's

it's   beautiful

FROZEN

Sound of summer garden . . .

I take it out and hold it in my hands
and
I can feel her head
its shape and texture and . . .
resilience

and I'm *flooded* with its   *Joy!!!* . . .

Birdsong, summer insects buzz . . .

and I say to the Mortician 'It's beautiful!'
and he just nods
because he knows it is
well, if anybody would know that he'd know that . . .
and after a while I give it to Ingrid
who says 'this fantastic brown it is'
and she holds it here

Her heart.

for a long time
and then she puts Rhona's witch stone
with it back in the box
and closes the lid.

Bigger box.
Ingrid takes the lid off.

different parts of her they managed to . . .
I thought top of the arm . . .
collar bone . . .
leg . . .

In there, we put a piece of gorse off
her nature table . . .
sheep wool wrapped in it . . .
place she *loved* to go to . . . windy hill . . .
daft really but . . .

also . . . Leo the Lion . . .
I go to the Chap . . . 'Guard her, keep her safe'
and we all smile.

And then . . . all the lids go back on.
He screws the lid back on the coffin
and I say
'Thank you.'
And he says 'No problem.
I wish more people could be doing this.'

She lights another cigarette. Agitated, angry, unsettled as . . .

then we come outside into this place.
Handy little parky garden place.
I feel at peace.
We're holding hands.
Me and . . . *bloody* Ingrid!

And she says . . .
'Now Mum . . . Be In The Moment'
I say 'What, Petal?'
She says 'Mum . . .
You're in a Very Bad Space.
You've Got To Let Go Of Your Anger.
You've got to Move On.
If You Hold On To Your Rage,
It Will Consume You.
Let It Go.
Make Space for Other Things To Enter Your Heart.'
She's got this new way of talking . . .
It's like listening to a Diet and Exercise Book.
I said 'What do you want me to do?'
. . . (that's how you talk back to them) . . .
and she said . . .
'I think what we Have To Do
is Forgive Ralph Wantage With Our Whole Hearts.'

I said 'I want to slap you
I want to spit in your face
I want to scratch you
I want to tear your eyes out with my . . .'

She said 'She's been dead for twenty years.
It's long enough.
Let Her Go.'

I said 'I just did, in there.'

I couldn't bear to look at her.

She said 'You should go and see him.
Tell him you forgive him.'

I said 'If I go to see him,
I'm taking a gun.
blow his brains all over the wall
I'm taking a knife
slice his thing off
stick the blade through his eye
and take out his brains that thought
what he thought to do what he did . . .
She was my little girl!'
And she said

Pause.

'So was I.'
Forgive that monster
I can't do that
How can I do that?
It's too much

It's too much
It's too much.

End of Act One.

161

Act Two

TWENTY
A PHONE CALL HOME

Agnetha, drink in one hand, cigarette in the other, circling a telephone. She is thinking about phoning . . . sometimes the decision is 'no,' sometimes it is nearly 'yes' . . . then, finally, it is, fuck it, 'yes' . . .

Agnetha
    Hi . . .
    Is that . . .
    Mary?
    . . . you sound like you're in a . . . *bathosphere* or something! . . .
    Do I? . . .
    No . . . I'm just in *London* . . .

English pronunciation.

Yeah . . .

Grand.

'The *Brit* Lecture'!
    yeah . . . the one David and I were gonna . . .
    it's . . . well . . . *kinda weird* . . .
    but . . . hey . . .
    Listen . . . how you doing? . . .

She listens.

    . . . well, you would . . . you will . . .
    ah, Mary . . . I know . . . I know . . .
    but . . .

She listens.

162

Mary . . . you just hafta be kind to yourself . . .
and . . . give yourself treats . . . and . . .
keep warm . . .
and . . . make everybody else look after you . . .
Even *The Kids*!
How are the . . .?
Give 'em a kiss from me, okay?
Hell . . . give 'em *Two!*

She takes a deep breath and . . .

Listen, Mary . . .
I've did a dumb thing . . .
I got drunk and . . .
I know I don't . . . I don't smoke either . . . that's
the *peculiar* thing . . .
but okay, I got . . . *major pie-eyed* and I . . .
sent an E-mail to David

and I'm frightened you got it

Oh
you . . .
listen . . . I'm *really* sor . . .
you must have . . .
I have to . . .
whaddya mean it made you *laugh?* . . .
Mary!!
Another woman sends your dead husband a
piece of *Hate* mail and
you *laugh??*
What kinda woman *are* you?

Beat.

So it didn't make you . . .
You didn't get . . .

Listens really hard . . .

It's just . . .
Mary . . . I really miss him

I played some footage of him
and . . . oh

yeah . . . with The Vicious Haircut . . .

Mary . . . you know I love you . . .

She listens.

Do you . . .?

She shakes her head . . .

Thank you . . .
that's . . .

Agnetha, away from the phone, bends over in agony.
Straightens, deep breath, and then . . .

I . . .
no, never mind . . .
listen . . .
I'll come see you when I get . . .
No . . . I haven't *met* anyone . . .
apart from serial killers . . .
This Brit Killer made me an offer I could refuse . . .
but hey, he's not dating at the present moment . . .

Listens.

. . . sure he's crazy . . .

What else is new with me . . .?

Mary . . .

Mary . . .

She lifts up her hand. The fingers are crossed.

Oh uh my cab's just pulled up
gosh it's early
I gotta go . . .
okay! . . .
yeah!
right!
You too.
Take Care!

Phone replaced. Pause. She watches as Nancy walks into a room somewhere.

Take Care.

Agnetha, leaving her personal detritus, assuming an authoritative demeanour, walks into the same room as Nancy . . .

TWENTY-ONE
TWO CARING WOMEN MEET

Nancy
　　I'm 'in a very bad space'
　　I know that.
　　And I need to 'move on'
　　I know that.
　　I know I'm ready.

Agnetha
　　How?

Nancy
　　He

She has to do this . . .

took her
she was going to Grandma's for me . . .

and he forced her into the van
and
she's ten
and
and he . . .
then he wrapped her in polythene sheeting
she was unconscious
but she wasn't dead then
he took her to a *shed* near
and
we *think* he sexually assaulted her
before he held the polythene on her face
and suffocated her.

She is short of breath.

Agnetha
Breathe.

Both inhale and exhale, hands on breasts, Nancy sort of following Agnetha . . .

Nancy
I'm accepting it.
I'm accepting she's dead.
But

Pause. Somehow an awful admission of guilt . . .

I'm not

and I need to

The same hand gesture of moving forward . . .

so
he's the   next step

I want to know *why.*
I want to know why *her.*

I want him to know what he's done.
I want him to know how I *feel*.
I want to *understand*.
If I could understand *why* . . . I might feel . . .
it might be . . . *better* . . . or even just bloody
different . . .
I might be able to . . .

For the third time, the hand gesture.

I've read all the data vis-à-vis the use of
Victim–Offender Communication in the
Treatment of Sexual Abuse and
Violent Crime Trauma . . .
My organisation is monitoring all the
Victim-Sensitive Offender Schemes Stateside . . .
Research-wise I'm impeccably prepared
I think my letters state that I'm up to
speed.
They said you could help.
Rubber Stamp It.
Fast-Track It.
It's Time.
I want a visit.

*Agnetha stands. Walks to the coffee machine,
thinking. Looks back at Nancy.*

Agnetha
Coffee?

*Nancy shakes her head. Agnetha pours two cups and
carries them into the next scene for . . .*

TWENTY-TWO
MY CHILDHOOD

Ralph and Agnetha, cup of hot coffee each. Sort of both off duty/role. Guard still there.

Ralph

. . . No . . . my *video* collection was in the *back* of the shed . . . my the *girls* were in the main body of the building . . .

Agnetha

but . . . *everything* . . . wrapped in polythene . . . right?

Ralph

oh yes

oh yes

Agnetha

and . . . filed?

Ralph

obviously

everything was in order

the whole layout made sense

if they'd *asked* me I'd've taken them through it methodically . . .

they needn't have . . .

going in mobhanded . . . they destroyed . . . the videos . . .

you're looking at about three thousand quid . . .

Agnetha

. . . but you see their point, Ralph . . .

Ralph

oh yes   still

coulda been more   *organised.*

Agnetha
No *remorse* then, Ralphie?

Ralph
Remorse. So what is that . . . remorse?

Agnetha
Like Regret. But more.
It's a feeling of . . . *compunction* . . .
of . . . deep . . . *regret* . . .
you *repent* your sin . . .
last cookie . . .

Ralph
last what?

Agnetha
last . . .

Remembers word.

. . . *biscuit* . . . last *biscuit*.
. . . split it?

Ralph nods. She splits the last biscuit and they share it as . . .

you feel . . .
sorrow
pity
compassion . . .
a sort of . . . *tender* feeling . . .

Ralph
I can't say I do.

Pause. Thinks.

The only thing I'm sorry about is that
it's not legal.

Agnetha
What's not legal?

Ralph
Killing girls.

Agnetha looks at her watch, picks up her writing pad, switches on her tape . . . business again.

Agnetha
Tell me about killing girls, Ralph.

Ralph
No.
It's Private.

Pause.

Agnetha
Tell me about your childhood then, Ralph.

Ralph
Big kitchen . . . we had a big kitchen obviously . . .
with filled cupboards . . . and shining work surfaces
. . . and that's where all
the kettles and pans . . . copper, all copper, all gleaming
in the light . . . because there were lights everywhere . . .
spotlights on tracking yeah . . . to just touch in a mood
of country . . . and a log fire . . . with them . . .
whatsis . . . *settles* . . .
wood . . . pine . . . antiquey . . . and here is where the
 dog sits . . .
lies . . . when he's not guarding . . . or going out on
 the hills
with us, *romping* . . . and then we come back and
 open the
tin of Pal Pedigree dogfood and he gets it, bosh, in
a special new shiny tin on the red stone floor . . .

Agnetha
What kind of dog is he, Ralph?

Ralph
Golden Retriever.
Pedigree. Kennel Club obviously.

Agnetha
What's his name?

Ralph (*pause*)
He doesn't have a name.
We don't go in for names.

Pause.

Lassie.

Agnetha
Tell me about your parents.

Ralph
Mother does the meals.
She goes to Safeways and Sainsburys and Tescos
and she gets a *variety* and she doesn't put up with
low standards . . .
oh no
oh no
the long pine table *always* has a selection of
. . . and the *correct* cutlery crockery for different
meals . . . and we all sit down to eat together . . .

Agnetha
And what does . . . Mother . . . cook for you all?

Ralph
Steakmasters . . . Oven Cook Chips . . . Viennettas . . .
After Dinner Mints . . . Hamlet Cigars . . .
Crusty Warm Bread.
Häagen-Dazs ice cream any many flavours . . . Mixed
Grills . . .

Agnetha
Is Father there?

Ralph
Yeah. Father. *Dad.*
Except when we're out riding ponies.
Or reading *poytry.*
In the room with all the books on shelves.
And the Nicam Digital television.

Agnetha
Any brothers or sisters, Ralph?

Ralph
No.
I'm an only child.
A much-loved only child.
Spoilt rotten.
But what can I do?

Agnetha (*regarding him for a time*)
Childhood's kinda private too, huh, Ralph?

Ralph
Yes
oh yes.

She picks up the biscuit plate. Crumbs on it. Carries it out past the Guard.

Agnetha
But we know you're a liar, Ralph.
And inconsistent.
We got a few crumbs from you.

She moistens a forefinger, starts picking up the biscuit crumbs, eating them, as . . .

little bits of you, cookie!
your mom pops you in the sink

stepdads arrive
you get chased
you get fucked
up your little bottom, don't you?
up your sad, dirty little ass . . .
we're onto you,
you sad, predictable, banal
fuck . . .

She realises she is eating his crumbs. She retches as . . .

'Memo.
Restorative Justice Lobby.
I would not be comfortable in
recommending Mrs Nancy Shirley
visit Ralph Wantage . . .'

TWENTY-THREE
THE SACRED ART OF FENG-SHUI

*Nancy, paint-spattered clothes . . . a splodge of white
paint ludicrously across her face . . .*

Nancy
Drip-Free Paint!
Liars!

It's big, this room
with everything out of it.
Spacious.
You can swing a cat in here now . . .

I'd swing that bloody American Doctor woman round
by her . . .

Quotes.

'The *experiment* is unviable!

173

the components *unstable*!'
Who does she think she *is*?

I've written some letters
made some phone calls
that's what you learn if you run an organisation . . .
Use The Right People!

I'll get that visit!

Whole house is bigger now . . .
Rhona's kiddie furniture gone
Bob's stuff . . .
I left a message saying 'Will I drop your stuff round?'
but he's lying low
sulking.
Only Ingrid speaks to me.

Nobody else.

They think what I want to do is . . . criminal . . .

Laughs.

So much for Families

Doesn't matter.

Bob was Yesterday's Newspapers for me anyway.

I said, 'I'm sorry, but how I felt about you
just hasn't survived . . .
it didn't keep . . . like something in the fridge . . . a
leftover . . .
in a jar . . . and when I picked it up . . . it was empty . . .
and he said 'Don't get *descriptive* with *Me!*
I could have set up with Marie from Nautilus
. . . why leave it till I'm nearly bloody *Past It?*'
I said 'Revenge, Probably' . . . but I don't mean that.
I don't mean him no harm.
I've got no malice in me.

No nothing.
Just   space
for
something   fresh
bit of . . . light
in the   red

bit of   fresh air
new   feelings

It hurts.

Once this visit's   I might go somewhere
I don't need to be here
nothing's keeping me

I'm free to go.

Sound of wings fluttering, not birds . . . Some
beautiful music plays . . .

TWENTY-FOUR
CONCLUDING MY ADDRESS

Agnetha at the lectern . . . large hall.

Agnetha
I spoke, in my preamble,
of myself as explorer . . .
of . . . navigating
the Arctic Sea of the criminal brain . . .
well the expedition is complete
what discoveries do we bring back from that alien
    terrain
to help make our own inner and outer landscape
warmer safer kinder better?
Cold comfort I'm afraid . . .
You see . . .

Most forensic psychiatrists tend to buy into the notion
    of evil.
I don't.
I can't.
I find no evidence that people are born evil.
To be evil is, dictionary definition, to be 'morally
    depraved.'
To my mind, that bespeaks having conscious control
over something.
The serial murderers I have tested are not in that
    category.
Their deeds themselves are bizarre grotesque
life-destroying
but not evil.
They are driven by forces beyond their control.
The difference between a crime of evil
and a crime of illness is the difference
between a sin and a symptom.
And I guess . . . as a moral society . . . as a
punishment society . . .
we can't let the notion of these deeds being
'symptoms'
intrude in the relationship between
murderers
and the rest of us
because
then we'd have to stop
and observe differently
the distinctions
between right and wrong
between the speakable and unspeakable
between the forgivable and unforgivable
the way sins do . . .

Agnetha moves away from the lectern . . .

But when you get back
   and you're   cold
   you're freezing yourself . . .
   you've got snow in your head . . .
   What then Dr Gottmundsdottir . . .
   What then Cookie?
   don't you cease to be an explorer
   and start . . .
   living there?

TWENTY-FIVE
THE VISIT

Prison visiting room. Ralph seated, Nancy at the entrance.
A guard.

Nancy (*to Guard*)

   That's him?

Guard nods . . . she goes to stand in front of Ralph.

   Ralph Wantage?

Ralph looks up. Barely nods.

   Nancy Shirley.
   You got my letter.
   You agreed to see me.
   Shall I sit down?

She does. For a long time, they look, they really look,
at one another . . .

Ralph
   She was your kid . . .
   One of them.
   This . . .

Nancy
Rhona.

Ralph
Rhona.
Funny you coming.

Pause.

Nancy
I want you to know
I forgive you for killing my daughter.

Silence. Ralph abruptly covers his eye sockets with both hands. Long pause. Guard watches Ralph. Nancy glances at Guard. Ralph brings his hands down, looks somewhere at the corner of her.
Very long pause . . . then the words sound very rusty . . .

Ralph
Thank you.

They sit for a time.

It's a nice day anyway.

Nancy
Yes.
There's buds out.
We saw a great *bank* of pussy willow on the way here.
I should have brought you some.
Are you allowed . . . that sort of thing?

He ignores her. He has no idea if he is allowed that sort of thing. Both glance at Guard. Guard nods. They both look away.

Ralph
We can have videos now.

Nancy

That's nice.
Is that nice?

Ralph

It's all right.

Long pause.

Nancy

I want you to know
I don't hate you.

Ralph

Okay.

Nancy

I used to.
But I don't any more.

Ralph

Okay.

Nancy

My daughter . . . Ingrid . . . said . . . Let It Go . . .
Like A Bird Into The Wind.
She's Spiritual.

Ralph

How old is she?

Nancy

Thirty-three

Ralph

Oh.

He is not interested.

Nancy

I've brought some photographs.
Would you like to see them?

Ralph
Of . . . her?

Nancy
Rhona.
And our family. Ingrid. Bob. My husband.

She gets them out. A small dog-eared selection.

Nancy
That's Rhona as a baby.

Hands them to him in turn . . .

That's me holding her.
This is Ingrid, that's her sister, holding her.
This is them holding their pets.
Her cat is Fluff.
Ingrid's holding Black-and-White.
You can see why they're called that . . . because she's
fluffy . . . and he's . . . see . . . ?
This is Rhona with Ingrid and my husband Bob.
We were on a day out.
I took it . . . it's uneven ground . . .
that's why they're slightly . . .

Her body indicates leaning . . .

This is Rhona dressed as an octopus.
For a fancy-dress competition.

Ralph
Did she win?

Nancy
She came third.
Behind Little Miss Muffet
and a Loch Ness Monster.

She points them out.

Ralph
She should have won.

Nancy
That's what we thought.
But we were biased obviously.

Ralph
That's good those arms.
How did you do them?

Nancy
She did them.
Rhona.
They're wire she made into springs.
When you touched them,
they . . .

Body language shivers and vibrates . . .

Ralph
I don't think I hurt her.

Nancy
You did.

Ralph
I don't think she was frightened at all . . .

Nancy
She must have been.

*Ralph thinks for a long time. Nancy watches him
carefully. When he looks up suddenly, she holds his
gaze. He looks away . . . she touches his arm . . .*

Ralph
You're not allowed to touch.

Nancy
Sorry.

Guard is watching. She removes her hand. Both sit back.

Nancy
But she must have been frightened!

Ralph keeps thinking . . .

Ralph
Do you live on a farm
and ride horses
and read poytry
and have warm bread?

Nancy
Not on a farm
No horses
We aren't particular big on poetry.
Books though.
Yes. Sometimes. Warm bread.
On cold days. You just pop it in the oven on
a low heat. Few minutes . . .

Ralph nods. He knew this.

Did your mother ever . . .?

Ralph
Oh yes
Oh yes.

She didn't.

Nancy
And your dad? What did he do?

Ralph
My dad
well
he was the disciplinarian
obviously.

Nancy
    Made you behave, did he?

Ralph
    Oh yes
    oh yes
    say you swore filthy language
    he's got you by the hair here

    Back of neck.

    and you're in the washing-up water
    bosh, wash your mouth out with soap water!
    or you done wrong
    anything!
    he's

    In Dad's voice.

    'See it in my eyes, twat?
    Can you see it, you fucking little pillock?
    I'm looking into you and I'm seeing shit!
    You keep yourself clean!
    You hear me?'

    Sound of a thump on flesh . . . Ralph registers it, side of head.

    You deaf little bugger!

    Another thump, same side of head. Ralph's body registers it.

    'You listening to me?
    Your head –

    Tap on forehead.

    taking this in?
    I'll make sure you hear what I say . . .
    Stand still

Stand still
Stand still
you stand still and don't move one muscle
not one
you don't even blink, twat,
until I know you know I mean what I say.
See it in my eyes, twat?'

Ralph is blinking rapidly.

Nancy
Frightening bugger.

Ralph nods.

Hurt you a lot?

Ralph, after a time, nods.

Can you see it hurt Rhona then?
Can you see it frightened her?
What you did.

Ralph thinks, impassive for a long time. Then . . .

Ralph
Yes.

He nods.
    Nods more times.
    Tears in his eyes.
    He wipes them fiercely. Violently.
    Dry painful sobs start.
    Awful, embarrassing, rusty crying.
    *Nancy watches. Guard watches. He holds his chest
in pain as he subsides. Calmly, she takes out a tissue.
Holds it up to Guard questioningly. He nods slightly,
dismissively. Nancy hands it to Ralph. He uses it. Puts
it on the table between them. Guard watches.*

Don't come and bother me again.
Cunt.

A pause. Then, a genuine apology . . .

Pardon my French.

Nancy exits. Guard stands over Ralph. Ralph stands, then walks in a circle round his cell.

TWENTY-SIX
LETTER-WRITING

Ralph, communal area, writing . . . interruptive loud music playing off centre . . .

Ralph
Dear Mrs Shirley . . .
Dear Nancy . . .
Dear Mrs Shirley . . .
I am writing to you . . .
I am sorry . . .
I am *very* sorry . . .
I am sorry . . .
I am sorry that I murdered . . .
I am sorry that I abused . . .
I am sorry that I . . .

turn the *fucking* music!!!
turn the *fucking* noise down!!!
You . . . Fuck! . . . down!!!

Down!

Bit of fucking *peace* . . . Jesus!

He aligns his stationery and pens into neatness. And again. And again.

I am sorry.
I am sorry from the bottom of my heart.

I am thinking about what I did.

I am thinking about what I did

I am realising

I realise in abusing and killing your daughter

. . . *Rhona* . . .

I   hurt   her

you

He realigns the paper . . . pen . . . envelope. And again.

Oh Christ.

He spits on the paper, folds it carefully, puts it in the envelope. Seals it. Tears it up. He starts to collect and align the torn pieces into a pile as . . .

Fucking Music!

TWENTY-SEVEN
SOMETHING AWFUL

Nancy, a cup of morning tea, a dressing gown . . . a sachet of resolve.

Nancy
Well!
Well!
Well . . . I'll go to sea on a duck's back!
Nancy Shirley!
Nancy Shirley how could you?
I've just done something *awful*!
I've been out on a *DATE*!

With a *Man!*
Roy Taylor!
Roy Taylor!
To a *Chinese Restaurant!*
Mince in *lettuce* leaves you eat with your fingers
and prawns in ginger and . . .
all this *washed down* with some sort of
Oriental wine
and I get tiddly and
you know what's coming next
he says 'Can I come in for a bit?'
and I say 'Lovely'
and next thing we're up there
doing . . . well . . . you can imagine!

Ingrid dropped by with this . . .
. . . 'Remorse' . . .

Looks closer.

. . . 'Resolve' . . . Resolve . . .

Ingrid says she understands

Which is more than I do!

She says, 'It's The Life Force'

The Wine Talking More Like!

I said, 'This isn't *Me* . . . Ingrid . . .'

She said, 'He's not bad-looking . . .'

I said, '*Please* don't tell your father!'

Life Force!

She talks such . . . *hocus pocus*!

TWENTY-EIGHT
QUIET AND SILENCE

*Agnetha and Ralph, prison room . . . a tape recorder . . .
notes. Agnetha closes her notebook.*

Agnetha
Well, Ralph. This is my last visit.
I wondered if you wanted to tell me anything more.
And I came to say 'Goodbye'

Ralph
Can you turn that thing off? (*Tape.*)

I've been wanting to tell you things I
don't want recorded, yeah?

Agnetha
Okay.

Turns off the tape.

Yes?

Ralph
I think I've caught something.
I think I caught cancer or something.
Here.
That's lungs right?
Lung cancer.
And that's me not even fucking smoking!

Agnetha
What does the doctor say?

Ralph
Says it's just Stress!
Fucking Shite!
Fucking Quack Cunt!

Stress is in here . . .

Forehead.

I know where
Fucking Stress Is!
This fucking *gnawing*. Here!

Chest.

Not Fucking Stress!

Agnetha
Where is this pain, Ralph?

He shows her . . .

That's your heart, Ralph.
Did the doctor check out your heart?

Ralph
Says there's nothing fucking *wrong*
with the heart!
Fucking Quack Cunt!

Agnetha
How long have you been in pain, Ralph?

Ralph
Er . . .
It started . . . night after that mother of that
girl Rhona I done came . . . that was Thursday . . .
so . . .

Counts on his fingers.

It's been a bit.

Agnetha
Mrs Shirley came to see you?
I recommended she . . .

Ralph

Yes, well . . . you were overruled by
The Doctor-in-Charge of Nutting-Off
weren't you?

Agnetha

And she visited with you?

Ralph

Yes.
She's forgive me, actually.
We're straight on it.

Spasm in his chest.

Oya
Oya
Oya.

Agnetha

I think you should talk to your doctor again.
Ask to see a psychologist.
What you are feeling may be psychological.
What you are feeling may be
Remorse.
And that will be very painful for you
Ralph.
Try rub it . . . here.

*She shows him on herself . . . middle of the chest, just
below the sternum.*

Ralph

Fucking hurts.
Burns.
Eats.
Gnaws.
Fucking Cancer.

Agnetha
Well. I'm sorry.
I hope they find out what it is and . . .
sort it out.
So.
This is Goodbye.

She stands.

Take care.
Bye Ralph.

To Guard.

Sue me.

Ralph tidies and realigns everything on the table top.
And again. And again . . .

Ralph
It's a question of finding a window
of opportunity
of always being ready
of always doing research
of committing yourself to
the rehearsal
the training
for practising
for when that
one golden moment
shines.
Oh yes
oh yes.

Beautiful, haunting music plays.

TWENTY-NINE
HOW HE DOES IT, WHY HE DOES IT

Ralph, in his cell, sweating, training gear. Working out.

Ralph
It's all a question of energy expended
vee calorie intake, yeah?
Fitness is what it's all about.
Which is twenty-per cent genetic
and eighty-per cent working at it yourself.
You can beat any condition if
you got a healthy body
oh yes
oh yes
fifteen
sixteen
seventeen eighteen
nineteen
twenty
yes!!!

*He drops. Unwinds a long cloth from round his neck.
Wipes the sweat from his brow, body. One of his
tattoos catches his eye. Looks at it carefully, fondly.*

Angels Fighting Devils.

Goes to a chair. Sits in it.

Fucking craftsman.

*He stands up, slings the cloth over the pull-up bar.
With his belt he fashions a noose. Stands on his chair.*

Gnawed to death?
I don't think so.

*He completes his preparations. Kicks the chair away
from him. He hangs, choking, jerking as . . .*

Hello
Hello
Hello
Hell
He . . .

A burst of wild, beautiful music plays . . .

THIRTY
GRAVESIDE

*Nancy, in a memorial garden. Some church-like music
off to the side comes to an end. Agnetha, entering,
watches her for a few seconds.*

Agnetha

Not a *big* funeral . . .

Nancy

Bit of a surprise . . . person with his talent for putting
sunshine in everybody's life . . .

Agnetha

I think the old lady in the black fur was his mother . . .

Nancy

His foster mother.

Agnetha

She looked . . . bad . . .

Nancy

Not as bad as if she had been his mother . . .

Agnetha thinks about this . . .

Agnetha
Yes. Yes.
I think that would be unbearable.

Nancy
Actually, nothing's unbearable.

Agnetha
You went to see him.

Nancy
And you tried to stop me.

Agnetha
I was trying to protect everybody.

Nancy
Him.

Agnetha
Everybody.

Nancy
Him.
How much time and energy did you give him?
And me?
And the others?
Cigarette?

Agnetha (*wants to, but . . .*)
I'm trying not to . . .

Nancy
Me too.

Puts hers away too.

You look upset.
Were you fond of Ralph?

Agnetha
It's not for Ralph . . .

It's for somebody else.
For me.

Nancy
Me as well.
I couldn't feel much for him really . . .

Agnetha
No.
It was . . .
not easy.

Both nod thoughtfully.

Nancy
Do you think he did it . . .
the . . . suicide . . .
Ralph . . .
because I went to see him . . .?

Long silence.

Agnetha
Yes.

Long silence.

Nancy
I don't know whether to be sad or glad.

Agnetha
Be both.

Nancy
No.
Bugger it.
I've been sad enough.
I'll be glad.
That murdering bugger's kept me from
happiness
and . . . laughing
and

cheer
for bloody twenty-odd years . . .
Bugger it.
Glad.
Laugh.
Have a joke.

Agnetha

My colleague and best friend,
David . . .
told jokes . . .

Nancy

Does he?

Agnetha

Did. Told. He died three months ago . . .
stupid accident . . .
wearing a seat belt . . .
observing the speed limit . . .
a truck goes out of control . . .
the driver is on crack . . .
the truck smashes the car . . .
the truck driver is unhurt.
David . . .

Nancy takes Agnetha's hand. Very matter of fact.

Anyhow.
Good joke from him.
These two lovers decide to commit suicide.
They both work in the same office.
So they put arsenic in their sandwiches . . .
go to work
twelve-thirty
they eat them.
It's a Suicide Pact Lunch.

Both women smile . . . laugh?

Nancy (*acknowledges*)
   Suicide Pact Lunch.

Agnetha
   I worked with him every day for ten years.
   Two days before he died . . .
   I slept with him.

   It just happened.

   His wife is a very good friend.

   Why am I telling you this?

Nancy
   Why are you?

Agnetha
   Do I tell her?

Nancy
   No.
   You just suffer.

   'The difference between a crime of evil
   and a crime of illness is the difference
   between a sin and a symptom . . .'

   Your words.

   I read your thesis . . .
   You knew what you were doing.
   Live with it.

   Nearby, the sound of doleful, funereal music from the
   crematorium chapel.

   Oh, perfect.
   Another funeral . . .!

   The sun breaks through, birds twitter, music plays,
   Nancy smiles at Agnetha.

   End of Play.

ILLYRIA

Illyria was first performed in the Cottesloe auditorium of the National Theatre, London, by the AII Project, Bristol, as part of the Connections season on 11 July 2002. The cast was as follows:

Lapin Sophie Alderson
Fabian Tom Bailey
Maria Vargas Clara Bin
Theresa Polly Carpenter
Feste Will Davies
Mary Sarah Forbes
Obseno Huwi Fraser
Flavia Sasha Frost
Magdo Jasmine James
Marie-Therese Carmel King
Violent Tom Lane
Madame Lucy Lowndes
Conrad Sammy Metcalf
Shoemaker Maise Platts
Andreas Joe Walkling

Design and Direction Paula Lees
Sound Sam Read
Lighting Philip Campbell
Stage Manager Laura Street
Music Tim Atack

Characters

Maria Vargas
journalist

Magda
translator

Marie-Therese
servant

Two Drivers

Theresa
servant

Mary
servant

Lapin
bureaucrat

Conrad
secretary

Fabian
soldier

Violent
soldier

Obseno
soldier

Feste
soldier

Andreas
soldier

Madame
a mistress

Flavia
a maid

Shoemaker

Man

Absolute bareness. Little as possible for props.
Maximum ingenuity.

Can be played by any number, any gender:
a psyche of wonderful colour only.

Music. Maybe some suggestion of dancing.

It goes dark.

A ragbag of people somewhere,
poorly but imaginatively dressed.

A pile of cases, boxes containing what is needed.

The place names and character names
can be changed for appropriate settings
of the company's choice: Bosnia, Vietnam,
Iraq, Ireland, Chechnya. Also, the date . . .

A young, smarter woman, shoeless,
shoes in hand, begins the story . . .

Maria
   Imagine
   in your awesome
   capacious
   and completely wonderful
   minds
   that it's early dawn
   it's dark as a tomb
   but you touch a switch . . .
   light

   Light.

   you touch another . . .
   heat

   Heat.

   you're going on a journey

   *She puts on her shoes
   as . . .*
      *Someone brings her a small flight bag, palm-top,
   camera perhaps . . .*

   you touch a switch . . .
   hot food . . .
   you have some hot chocolate

   *Someone comes with hot chocolate . . . the smell of it
   pervades . . .*

   perhaps some hot toast with butter . . .

Someone comes with delicious toast, butter . . .
again the smell of it pervades . . .

and you're about to take a bite . . .
when . . .

She suddenly vomits . . . hugely . . . People attend . . .

Maria
Shit!

Then vomits again.

Shit!

Someone wipes her face.

It's time to go
passport
tickets
money

They arrive for her. It is most efficient. Ordered.
Meanwhile, she dresses for travel . . . puts her
documents, camera etc., in safe places . . .

you're going to another country.

Someone makes jet noise, using a ghetto-blaster . . .
decks . . . whatever . . .
    He picks up her luggage . . . she walks into special
light.

Someone (*from the listeners*)
What country, friend, is this ?

Maria
This is Illyria, Lady.

Jet noise magnifies . . .

Maria
Illyria.

Not your country.

Decks play appropriate sounds.
   A young woman greets her with a handshake.

Magda
   Magda.

Maria
   Maria.

Magda
   Illyrian.

Maria
   British (*or place of origin*).

Magda
   Interpreter.

Maria
   Perfect!

   They laugh.

Magda
   One child. Girl. Husband.
   Welcome.

Maria
   Thank you.

Magda
   We go this way.

   Magda collects Maria's bags.

Maria
   Imagine.

Magda
   Illyria.
   Once famous beautiful green green woods.

Maria
Yes.

Magda
Once music. (*She sings.*)
Once beautiful dancing. (*She dances.*)

They both smile . . . laugh . . . beautiful music plays.

Now
famous for War
you come for our War . . . ?

Maria
Yes.

Magda
Sorry.

They both shrug.
    It's a pity. They are driven. People create the
landscape they pass through . . . they have only
themselves and junk to do this . . .

Maria
You're being driven into a city
that was once home to
say, four hundred thousand people
now home to War
Imagine

Magda
devastation . . .

She points it out. Helpful.

Maria
beyond imagining . . .
shells and bombs have collapsed
the apartment blocks into
grey concrete

Magda
  grey concrete sandwiches

Maria
  you're being taken . . .
  our official car . . .
  bucks and tips
  between the heaps of rubble
  the deep craters . . .

Magda
  bombs

Maria
  for mile upon mile there is
  no building left intact . . .

Magda
  Different, eh?
  from your country?

Maria
  Yes.
  How old's your girl?

Magda
  Baby.

  Shows Maria photograph.

Both
  Aaah!
  Lovely!

Maria
  You leave the remains of
  the city
  then through the green green woods
  we drive

Magda
    long way
    beautiful, ah?

Maria
    you watch her wind down the window

Magda
    air!
    country!
    woods!

Maria
    and a crack
    like a branch breaking
    and

Magda slumps onto Maria's lap.

    it's
    taken her life
    most of her head
    is gone . . .

Maria cradles Magda's body as . . .

    We drive on.

    Picture
    arriving at your destination.

Drivers
    Out! Out!

The Drivers separate Maria from Magda . . .

Maria
    No! Please! Wait! No!

They dump her, her bags, out of the car. They vanish.

Maria
    Where am I?

Off, we hear three female voices raised in fierce debate.

Marie-Therese
It's true!

Theresa
It's not true!

Marie-Therese
It is!

Theresa
It can't be!

Maria
It is not a language you speak . . .

*They enter: Marie-Therese, Theresa and Mary.
Considerable women . . . they will be doing all the
work here . . . They have scrubbing brushes, water,
soap . . . vestiges of modern cleaning equipment.*

Mary
Ya dung beetle with your little piles
of snot and shit you made it up . . .

Marie-Therese
I made nothing up!
It is the shining truth!

*They start unpacking equipment, aprons on, rubber
gloves, sleeves up, as . . .*

Theresa
It is not the shining truth!

Marie-Therese
I swear by all the saints in heaven
all the angels on their clouds
and on the graves of my beloved father
and mother . . .

Theresa
> All the saints in heaven and all the
> angels on their clouds and your
> beloved mother and father in their
> graves are as big liars as you are then . . .
> rolling little piles of dirt together
> and sticking them
> together with
> your snot and shit . . .
> dung beetle!

They look at Maria.

Maria
> Journalist. (*Mime.*)
> Foreign. (*Mime.*)

She's not worth any effort. Big display of disdain.
> *She's pond-life.*
> *Back to reality . . .*
> *Marie-Therese is the best storyteller in the world,*
> *who drives Theresa crazy, Mary, who listens . . . They*
> *begin to build the house . . . a shell only, half a wall,*
> *a staircase leading nowhere . . . cupboards as . . .*
> *Marie-Therese gets into her narrative stride.*

Maria
> They ignore me.

Marie-Therese
> Anyway
> they took her at dead of night
> from her own bed!
> They pushed her old mother
> viciously in her old breast!

Mary
> Ay yi yi . . .

Marie-Therese
and her father they clubbed
like this! and this!
with the hard butts of their rifles!

Theresa
Oh . . .

*Theresa always tries to resist her stories, is always
drawn in against her will . . .*

Marie-Therese
In the back of the truck
on the way to prison
they took turns
the soldiers
in fondling her!

Mary
God in Heaven . . . Holy Mother!

Marie-Therese
Every night . . . in the prison . . . she's
lying bound and gagged and with a
hood covering her face . . . one guard
came and . . .

She demonstrates what he did.

Mary
The same one?

Marie-Therese
The same one.

Theresa
How could she tell it was the same one?

Marie-Therese
By his smell!
Every day . . .

they would take her down to the basement
lie her on a bloodstained bed . . .
electrocute her with probes . . .
here . . . (*gums*)
here . . . (*nipples*)
and here . . . (*vagina*)

Other Two
Ayeeh!

Marie-Therese
One day
they take her down to the basement
lie her on a bloodstained bed
take off her hood
on the next bed
is her fiancé!

Mary
God in Heaven Holy Mother!

*The shell of the house is now there . . . The three
women clean, polish, scrub and spray as . . .*

Marie-Therese
The torturer comes in with a
little tabby kitten . . .

Other Two
Aaaah!

Marie-Therese
and a bag of sacking tied at the top
he puts the kitten on her breast
it purrs
he opens the bag
takes out a poisonous snake!

Other Two
Ay!

Marie-Therese
  He puts the kitten in an oil can
  this big with an open end
  this open end he puts here (*vagina*)
  at the other end of the oil can
  is a smaller hole
  he puts the snake in the hole
  closes the hole
  then he starts to heat up the oil can
  both animals are terrified
  trapped
  pursued by the heat
  the snake moves towards the kitten . . .
  the kitten . . . where can the kitten go?
  it is wild with fear
  it scratches it claws
  the kitten crawls into
  her . . . (*vagina*)
  the snake follows
  she screams as she feels inside her . . .

Theresa
  Oh!

Mary
  Holy Mother!

Marie-Therese
  She faints dead away.

  Her fiancé, forced to watch
  all this time
  screams and screams and screams
  he is clubbed unconscious
  carried away
  she never sees him again!

Mary
  God in Heaven!

Theresa
Holy Mother!
The poor poor man!

Mary
It's true?

Marie-Therese
As true as I stand here.
It happened in Castilia
where my mother's aunt lives.
It's all over town.
Everyone keeps quiet.
There!

The space is ready. It really is clean, sparkling . . .

Maria
It's a building
still standing
an old house
in a clearing
in the green green woods
once pleasing of shape
once beautiful of design
it is guarded by soldiers.

Three young men, Violent, Obseno, Fabian, enter as soldiers.

What house is this?

They freeze.

Marie-Therese
Journalist.
Foreign.

Three men do another pantomime of disdain.

Obseno
This is a Safe House, Lady.

Maria
  A what?

Maria, Marie-Therese, Theresa, Mary stand still,
submissive, as soldiers check place out . . .
Decks do appropriate sound . . . Light panel similar.

Violent (*public*)
  It's a house just a house
  a regular normal house
  it's regular normal but but but but

They fan out, guarding, but . . .

Fabian (*private*)
  . . . but the kitchen

He's there, the kitchen of his darkest nightmare . . .

  stain here on the floor
  no amount of scrubbing can remove
  it's the shape of a body
  but the head is some way off
  the ice box holds many packs
  of unidentifiable joints of meat
  labelled simply 'Hostage 99'
  labelled clearly 'Hostage 99'.

They try to keep it together. Brave but but but . . .

Violent (*public*)
  It's a ruin just a ruin
  a regular normal ruin
  check it out it's regular normal
  a ruin but but but . . .

Obseno (*private*)
  but the bathroom

He's there . . . worst nightmare . . .

a mark in every basin
as if the tap flows blood
and the plumbing clinks and clanks
reminiscent of a code
when you flush the handle sticks
then there's such a stench
it's foul and sweet like pork gone off
and no cleanser can remove it
no cleanser can remove it.

Keep it together . . .

Violent (*public*)
it's bricks it's stone it's shit
regular normal shit
check it out it's normal shit
but but but . . .

Fabian
. . . the staircase

He's there. Hell.

Obseno (*private*)
when you climb in the direction 'up'
you feel you're going down
and despite the sun through windows
you think it's cold and dark
and halfway up a hand of wind
clutches at your sleeve
you turn, there's no one there
you turn, there's no one there

Fabian (*public*)
it's air it's open air
regular normal air
check it out there's open air
but but but . . .

Violent
> . . . the bedrooms
> when you open any wardrobe
> all the clothes feel warm
> among the pairs of shoes
> are pairs of feet
> coat-hangers clink like skeletons on a gibbet
> and when we fall asleep
> we sleep on dead men's hands
> we sleep in dead men's hands
> we are tossed there in our sleep
> so we never fall asleep
> we never fall asleep . . .

He really loses it. Fabian and Obseno get him against a wall. Shove him, tough him up . . .

Obseno
> Check it out . . . awake!
> Check it out . . . alert!

Fabian
> So we never fall asleep
> so we never fall asleep!

Violent (*toughed up*)
> We never fall asleep . . .

The house is clear of anything but dread. They take up guard positions.

Maria
> In this house
> no switch for
> light
> no switch for
> warmth
> but someone keeps this house
> running . . .

The sound of a helicopter hanging over the house . . .

Mary
Madame!

Marie-Therese
Already?

Theresa
Quick!

They repack their cleaning equipment tout suite . . .

Marie-Therese
I'm worn out.

She might have done no more than put on her gloves while exhausting herself with storytelling.

Theresa
I'm sure!

Mary
Quick . . . quick!

Theresa
We're ants.
Build a city of snotballs
wash the snotballs
scrub the snotballs
lay eggs
reproduce
and all for what?
Some Fat Queen Ant!

They are standing ready when Lapin, middle management in a suit, arrives.

Marie-Therese
It's Lapin!

Theresa
Speaking of snotballs . . .

Mary
Shhhh!

Lapin terrifies them. They hate her.

Lapin
Madame is on her way.
She will be very tired.
All this dodging from one
hole to the next.
So fatiguing!
This is her room?

They nod. They talk to Lapin as little as possible.

Everything shipshape?

I hope so . . .

*She walks around, checks every detail. It's a job and
it's a game . . .*

Fine
good
perfect

They relax a bit . . .

polished

neat

delightful . . .

They relax more . . .

apart from the smell.

Gotcha . . .

there is a rank odour of
peasant sweat
that I do not think
Madame will care for at all . . .

She waits while the three find some battered cans of fresh-air spray, spray it around . . . the smell pervades.

Fine
good
but let's stop it at the source.
Mmm???

Marie-Therese takes a used deodorant out . . . they take turns.

Good.
One more time for you I think . . . (*Mary.*)

Mmmm
Better
Go and bring Madame to her
new room while you're still fresh!

They go, muttering . . .

Marie-Therese
One day
I'll have polished the floor
so shiny so slippery
when Lapin steps on it
she'll slide
like a billiard ball
cannon off that wall
onto the banister
off the banister onto the wall
wall banister
banister wall
foot of the stairs
where she'll lie
every bone snapped like a pretzel
screaming for help
I'll continue polishing . . .

Theresa can top this . . .

Theresa
One day
I'll be bleaching the sheets
in the big boiler
Lapin'll bend over to
inspect the whiteness of the sheets
she'll tip right over
helped by the sharp whack
I'll give to her shins
with the stick I use for
tamping down the sheets
I'll tamp her down till
she's as clean and white
as my sheets
then I'll hang them and her
out on the line
where they will flap
and she will moan
and I'll pray for a good drying wind . . .

Can Mary top this . . . ?

Mary
One day
One day
I'll be . . .

Lapin behind her . . .

Lapin
Be what?
Anything but servers?
Anything but scrubbers?
Anything but complainers
snivellers
moaners?

Mmm?
Mmmm?
Mmmmm?
Anything but whingeing whining
Women???
Get!!!

They get . . .
    Lapin puts on white gloves as . . .

they had a party
in the kitchen courtyard
they made pies
a lot of wine
asked all the soldiers
all the guards
even the double agent
everybody knows is a double agent
not me
I put on my blue
just in case
sat in my room
no invitation
no come down have a good time,
Lapin.
Well, I don't want affection
respect!
I'm a woman with a position
not a lot can say that
everyone got drunk
did things in the wine cellar
not me
I dozed off
creased my blue.
No one'll get anything on me.

She sees Maria . . .

Who are you?

Maria
Journalist. (*Mime.*)
Foreign. (*Mime.*)
I've come to meet Madame. (*Mime.*)

Lapin
Madame will pee her exquisite silk
designer underwear with
pleasure.

*Accompanying mime conveys only Madame's polite
pleasure. Soldiers smirk.*

Maria
Good.
Thank you.
Can I get an interpreter?
The last one . . . Magda . . . she was . . . she died . . .

Her words are lost in noise.
  Decks create . . .

Maria
A dusty armoured limousine
motorcycle outriders
an air of frenzy
scorches into the courtyard
gravel sprays like sniper fire . . .

Everyone to attention . . .
  *Two more soldiers, Andreas and Feste . . . twanging
like piano wires with tension . . .*

Andreas
Fuck!

Feste
Fuck!

Andreas
Check! Fuck!

Feste
Yes! Yes! Fuck!

Andreas
Okay.
Cool.
Get the Bitch in!
Get the Bitch in!

Feste
Keep your hair
. . . on your head!

Fuck!

*Madame arrives, carried carefully by the three women
in their white gloves. Supervised by . . .
Madame is beautiful, very young, and cocooned in
layers of expensive cloths, pashminas, silken: rather
like a huge bug.
Secretary Conrad has accompanied her.*

Conrad
We had to have the bulletproof
shields up all the way!

Flavia
Careful!

Lapin
Careful . . . Careful!!!

Feste
Yes, miss. Careful!

Conrad
  Lie down on the floor going
  through towns!

Flavia
  Gently!

Lapin
  Gently . . . Gently!!!

Andreas
  Gentle . . . Gentle!

Conrad
  They shot at the tyres . . . we've
  been driving on flat tyres for
  the last twenty kilometres!

Lapin
  Take off her . . . take it off!!!

*The three women gently unwind the bug from its
cocoon, revealing an exquisite, beautifully dressed,
beautifully painted toy of a woman.*

All
  Ooooooh!

Marie-Therese
  Oh!

Theresa
  Beauty!

Mary
  Tired!

Conrad
  Hot!

Flavia
  See to her!

Lapin
See to her . . . See to Her!!!

They administer to her as . . .

Flavia
our moth!
are her wings crushed?
are her colours dulled?
can she still land upon
a leaf?
sip nectar from
a flower?
Our moth!

Maria
Imagine.
You are in the wrong place.
You have been brought to the wrong place.
This is not who you've come to see.
You've been brought,
by some terrible error
to
the most powerful woman
in Illyria.

Madame stands impassively.
  They comb her hair.
  Arrange her.
  Stand back.
  Look at her.
  Wait.
  Finally, in a small, babyish, carrying voice . . .

Madame
Mirror.

Flavia
Mirror.

They bring her a mirror.
    She looks in it.
    No expression.

Madame
    My lips

Marie-Therese paints her lips.

Mirror.

Flavia
    Mirror.

They bring the mirror again, she looks in it.

Madame
    Yes.

Madame is ready . . .

Everybody stared at the car!
all along the road
which The Generalissimo had
cleared for me!
so we could go fast!
The people
just stood and stared at the car
just to catch a glimpse of me!
I sat up very straight
so they could see me
so my back is very
tired . . .

All
    Ooooh . . .

They rush to sort this out.

Madame
    They like to see me
    I'm much prettier than The Wife!

Maria
You have papers to meet
The Wife!

Madame
When she travels he doesn't
even order the car polished
that's how little he cares
for her!!!

At one turning the car
slowed down
and there was a young man
with dark eyes looking in
as near as I am to you,
Lapin . . .

Lapin bows.

Lapin
Madame.

Madame
and he met my eyes
and he leaned forward as if he
was going to kiss the bulletproof
window
and then he spat!

One of the outriders caught him
I'm going to have him hurt
for that!

Marie-Therese
Spat?

Theresa
At her?

Mary
Why?

Conrad
Tide's turning?

Lapin
What's going on???

When Madame looks again, all is silence and respect.

Madame
I wish The Generalissimo was here.

Marie-Therese
Oh . . .

Theresa
There, there . . .

Mary
So in love!

Madame
I want to know when he's coming.

Flavia
Madame wants to know when he's coming.

Lapin telephones.
  Andreas and Feste have a cigarette.

Andreas
Fuck! Fucking fuck!

Feste
Look at the hands! Fucking hands!

Andreas
Nearly wet-trouser job!

Feste
Nearly fucking brown-trouser job!

Andreas
Jesus Christ!

Both burst out laughing.
    Stop as Maria is near them.

Feste (*quietly*)
Good bum.

Andreas (*same*)
Great tits.

Has to be quite silent and hidden as . . .

Maria
You wish you were a man.

Marie-Therese
If the crowd's against
her . . .

Theresa
spitting

Mary
if she's not popular . . .

Violent
spitting?

Obseno
shooting out tyres?

Andreas
activity?

Madame
I must sit down.

Flavia
Madame must sit down.

*Mary fetches a chair for her. It arrives in place as
Madame lowers herself.*

Conrad
No salutes

Lapin
no salutes

Feste
no salutes . . . no salutes!

Madame
I'm hot.

Theresa fans her . . .

Conrad
No cheers

Lapin
no cheers

Fabian
no cheers . . . no cheers!

Madame
I want to rest until My Beloved arrives.

Flavia
Madame wants to rest until Her Beloved arrives.

The three women create a sumptuous bed for her.

All
Our moth!
are her wings crushed?
are her colours dulled?
has someone lit a candle?
has she flown too near the flame?
Our moth?

Madame
I want to be asleep now!

Flavia
Madame wishes to be asleep now!

Marie-Therese
Shhh . . .

Theresa
hush now . . .

Mary
there there . . .

Lapin brings a pill box.

Marie-Therese
Aaagh!

Theresa
Poison?

Mary
so soon?

Conrad
are you sure?

Lapin (*contemptuous*)
sleeping pill!
Just one.

Madame takes a pill.

Madame
It's not working
they never work
these pills you give me
I'm always awake!

She is asleep.
They put her to bed. Arrange her.

All
Our moth!

234

are her wings crushed?
are her colours dulled?
is the summer over?
is there frost on every leaf?
Our moth!

Lapin
Leave.

Three women leave . . .

(*To Flavia.*) Leave. Leave!

Leaves.

Conrad
I missed you.

Lapin
No, you didn't. The telephone's dead.
The telex isn't working.

Crosses to window . . .

Lapin
Guards still guarding . . .
they're our guards . . .
that's Fabian . . . who at the servants' party
was sick in the . . . or so I heard . . .

Conrad
I love you.

Lapin
No, you don't.

He starts to touch her.

Conrad
Listen . . . the only thing there is to life
is waking up fucking working eating
going to bed fucking and sleeping . . .

let's do one of those now then.
I know! . . . fucking!

Lapin
The only thing to do therefore is to
wake up in the best place get the
best fucking work in the best place
eat the best food go to bed in the
best bed lie down in the best place . . .

Conrad
You're right.
Let's practise.

Lapin
No babies.

Conrad
Deal.

Lapin
Protection?
Show me.

He shows her a condom.

Conrad
So romantic . . . what happened to
green green woods
music
dancing . . .?

Lapin
Be quiet.

She leads him to a secluded spot.
    *Violent and Obseno take up positions where they
can watch.*

Violent (*whispered*)
Live Sex Show.

Obseno (*same*)
Entertainment for the Boys!

Everyone aware of the sex going on . . .
Meanwhile, a mime exchange?

Fabian
Quick man. Working woman.
No time to . . .

Mime for 'hang about', 'do foreplay'.

Maria
I have been brought to the wrong place.
I was to talk to the Generalissimo's Wife.
Not . . .
Do you understand?

Fabian
British?

Maria
Journalist.

Fabian
Sweetheart?

Maria
Husband. Sort of.

Sex scene and onlookers hot up. Mirth as . . .

Violent
Go on!
Give it to her!

Obseno
Hard!
Do It!

Fabian
Wartime. Fast time.

Maria vomits . . .

Fabian
Bad food?

Maria
Pregnant.
Baby.

Lapin returns.

Lapin (*to Fabian*)
Clean that up
now.
Now!

Maria
Thank you.

Lapin (*to Maria*)
I want to wake
up in her place have her work
and her food and go to bed in
her bed and fuck how she fucks
and sleep where she sleeps

Conrad returns to applause from soldiers . . .

get one high up as possible
keep the others off.

Maria
I understand.

Lapin
American?
Journalist?
I doubt it.

Maria
Anyone speak English . . . ?
Translate . . . ?

Conrad
I do.
Many talents.

*Telephone rings . . . telex . . . communications
operative . . .*

Lapin (*to telephone*)
Yes?
Yes.
Yes.
No.
Yes.
Yes.

Phone down.

The Generalissimo is on his way!

*Klaxons, alarms . . . Soldiers to attention . . . Three
women rush in . . .*

Marie-Therese
It's true!

Theresa
It's not true!

Marie-Therese
It is!

Theresa
It's not!

Lapin
The Generalissimo is on his way!

Women
Shit!

Huge activity from everybody.

Feste
Never stops! Fuck!

Andreas
He's there!
He's here!
Move!

Violent
What's that?
Check that!
Check *that*!

Feste
Move it!
Move it!

Obseno
Palaver!
Fucking palaver!

Andreas
Fucking *fast*!

Fabian
Doing it!
Doing it!

Feste
Move it!
Move it!!!

Obseno
Yes!
Yes!
Yes!!!

As . . .

   Martial, victorious music plays, bunting . . . flags are hung . . . security checked . . . uniforms . . .

Large portrait of The Generalissimo is hung.

Lapin
Wake her up,
get her ready.

Flavia
Wake her up,
get her ready..

Lapin
Here we go
puppet show
the puppet with the hole
for the puppet with a stick.

*She watches impassively as the women wake up
Madame, strip her, wash her, perfume her, dress her in
conspicuously unwearable beautiful sexual garb.*

Maria
Can I talk to her?

Conrad
Wait.
Enjoy our favourite occupation.
Waiting.

They watch the women working.

Women's work.

Not you. Journalist.

Writing. Thinking. Clever.

These. Carthorses.

Marie-Therese
Anyway
this man would lie in wait
for women in their own houses!

Mary
Oooh!

Marie-Therese
In that town they used to leave their
doors open but when this started happening . . .

The story wafts into Madame's ears as . . .

Mary
Aye!

Marie-Therese
even so, he'd find a way in . . . under a
shutter . . . thin knife . . . in the latch . . . and
he'd be waiting . . . hiding!

Theresa
Oh . . . now . . .

Marie-Therese
and then he'd come . . . knife in hand
and hold it to their throat!

Theresa
God in Heaven!

Mary
Holy Mother!

Marie-Therese
He'd turn them over . . . off with their . . .
and stick it in . . . the back!

Mary
In the back?

Marie-Therese
In the back
then he'd turn them over and
make them suck his . . .

Other Two
Aye!

Marie-Therese
then he'd leave
taking all the money from their purse
one of them got up after it all
went out on the street
it was pitch-black
she saw someone coming towards
her
she called for help
he came close to her
it was him!

Theresa
Oh!

Mary
No!

Marie-Therese
and he came in and did it again!

Both
Again?

Marie-Therese
Again!

Theresa
God in Heaven!

Mary
Holy Mother!
It's true as I stand here.
It happened in Forniccia where my
sister's best friend lives.
It's all over town.

They haven't caught him yet.
There!

Madame is dressed.

Madame
Mirror.

Flavia
Mirror.

Madame
Yes.
I look beautiful.

Rest
Yes, Madame.

Madame
I look perfect.

Rest
Yes, Madame.

Madame
The Leader
my Beloved
will be hungry when he arrives
from protecting the country.

Maria
She wears
Versace Ferrigamo
Tiffany Manolo Blahnik.

Conrad
She wears
Money Money
Money Money . . .

*The three bring a table, arrange it with fruit, wine,
flowers, etc. A feast for the Generalissimo. Madame
surveys it.*

Madame
Yes.
Go.

Flavia
Go.

The women go.

Madame
Any message for me?

Lapin
He is on his way.

Madame
Anything else?

Lapin
He cannot wait to reach your side
and hold your exquisite body
in his strong arms.

Madame
He loves me so much.

Lapin
Madame.

*Madame sits quite still, while Lapin reviews the
meal . . . eats a grape . . . smells a flower . . . tries the
rustle of a cigar etc., bouquet of the wine . . .*

Madame
Not poisoned?

Lapin
No, Madame.

Madame
Haaah!

Lapin
Bored, Madame?

Madame
No.
I'm far too much in love.

Lapin
Madame.

Madame
Lapin . . . ?

Lapin
Madame?

Madame
I keep thinking about . . .
holes.

Maria
You keep thinking
about . . .
holes . . .

Lapin
Holes?

Madame
Holes.

Pause.

Lapin
Would you like me to read the
Generalisssimo's love
letters to you?

Madame shakes her head.

Would you like to write a love letter to the
Generalissimo?

Shakes head.

a manicure?

a pedicure?

a massage?

Madame shakes her head.

Lapin
A foreign journalist bitch is
here to make up lies about you . . .

Both look at Maria. Polite mimes all round.

Madame
I think I'd like to see my shoes.

Lapin
But The Generalissimo will be
arriving shortly . . .

Madame (*screaming*)
I'm Madame, the Generalissimo's
beautiful mistress and you do
what I want!

Lapin goes to the telephone.

Lapin
Madame would like to see her shoes.

Flavia
Madame would like to see her shoes.

Lapin
Madame would like to see her shoes.

Soldiers bring on large cases. Three Women take out pair after pair of beautiful, useless shoes and lay them out in rows of pairs as . . .

Marie-Therese
It's true.

Theresa
It's not true!

Marie-Therese
It is!

Mary
It can't be!

Madame listens . . .

Marie-Therese
Anyway
he came home
and he had been drinking all day long!

Theresa
Oh!

Marie-Therese
and his mind was gone with the wine
but his body was as powerful as a
bull's!
she was sitting in the chair
and the children were all
asleep in their beds!

Mary
Ah!

Marie-Therese
He slapped her this way
across her face
and that way across the face!

Theresa
God in Heaven!

Mary
Holy Mother!

Marie-Therese
and then he took his cigar
from his mouth and burned her
here
here
and here

Theresa
brute

Mary
the pig

Marie-Therese
and then he took the bread knife
off the table
and he slit her nostrils
and the blood ran down her cheeks
like tears
and he laughed!

Theresa
He laughed?

Marie-Therese
He laughed!
and the sound of his mad laughter
awoke the children
and he turned with the breadknife
in his bloody hand and
started towards the stairs!

Theresa
God in Heaven!

Mary
Holy Mother!

Marie-Therese
She clung to his trousers
desperately trying to stop him
but he went on and on
up and up
to the bed where the children lay

Theresa
and then . . .

Mary
there they were . . .

Marie-Therese
there they were
crying piteous tears
and he gutted them
from the oldest
to the littlest baby
one after the other
and then he let the knife fall
and that poor mother turned
that knife upon her own
miserable broken heart!

Theresa
God in heaven!

Mary
Holy Mother!
It's true?

Marie-Therese
As true as I stand here
It happened in Manzinnia
where my second cousin's old

schoolteacher lives.
He was a member of the government.
Everybody keeps quiet.
There!

There is a row of shoes as far as the eye can see . . .
curving . . . snaking across the stage . . .

Madame
Let her come and see my shoes.
Let her see how much the
Generalissimo loves me!

Flavia
Let her come and see Madame's shoes.

Conrad
Madame invites you to see
her beautiful shoes . . .

Maria
Madame.
Maria Vargas . . . I'm a . . .

Madame
These are from New York.

Conrad (*translating*)
These are from New York.

Madame
These are from Italy.

Conrad
These are from Italy.

Madame
They are made of wild deer hide.

Conrad
They are made of wild deer hide.

Maria
I'd like to ask Madame about her
feelings about the state of constant
war in her country . . .

Conrad
Foreign journalist wonders how may
pairs of shoes you have . . .

Madame
I don't know.
Let me think.
Let me look.

Conrad
Madame does not talk about politics.
She prefers shoes.

Maria
They are very beautiful.
But does she not want a state of peace . . .
where everyone has shoes
. . . a safe place for her shoes?
what does she think of conditions
where everybody is living in fe –

Conrad
Foreign journalist wonders
how you keep all
these shoes in such good
condition . . .

Madame
I only wear them.
I do not do . . . polishing!
the foreign journalist is not
very interesting!
I want to wear these.

Flavia
Madame wants to wear these.

*The three women run forward with chair, shoehorn,
willing hands . . .*

Conrad
Madame is tired with your
questions.

Maria
Perhaps we could talk later.

Conrad
Perhaps.

Maria
Perhaps with another translator.
Translating is so fatiguing.

Conrad
Perhaps.
What a shame you do not have
our language.

*Maria stares at him.
Then . . .*

Maria
Everybody pretends to know
what's going on.
Nobody knows what's going on.
There's everything to do.
There's nothing to do.
Nothing's dangerous.
Everything's dangerous.
Your only story so far
is that death next to you
in the car . . .
Everyone's just

waiting
for a pull
from a
taut string
a long long way off . . .

Telephone rings . . . communications . . . Everyone
jerks on that long taut string . . .

Lapin (*telephone*)
Yes?
Yes.
No.
Yes. (*out*)

The Generalissimo has been delayed.

Nothing.

Why?
Delayed.
Why?
A change of plan.
Why?

Maria
The atmosphere changes
in a heartbeat

Lapin and Conrad check the window . . . everybody
running around, headless chickens.

Lapin
The guards are still there!
The guards are still there!

Conrad
Can you see their faces?
Can you see their uniforms?

Lapin
I can't see!
I don't recognise them!
They're not in uniform!

Conrad
Not a delay!

Lapin
A reverse!
A reverse!

Feste
Fuck!
Knew it!
All the way here!

Andreas
Fucking peasant villages
faces giving it 'Wait, just wait!'
Fuck!

*They start to take down the bunting, flags . . . the
large portrait of The Generalissimo is ripped to shreds
as . . .*

Marie-Therese
It happened
last time
just like this
the people cut at the wires
men with gardening shears
and women with kitchen knives
the wires curled back
they rushed through and up
the wide sweeping steps
of the house itself
the fat cats were sitting inside . . .

Andreas
Fuck.
Fuck!

Feste
Lost It!
Fucking Lost It!!!

They start taking off badges, tags, distinguishing signs, as . . .

Marie-Therese
Their powerful foreign friends
were powerless to do anything.

Conrad (*to Maria*)
You must be very
careful.
You must be very quiet.
You must record nothing.

Marie-Therese
The fat cats
wet from their own wee
soiled from their own shit
watch the visitors
the garden shears and the
kitchen knives
raise
plunge
again and again
the fat-cat blood ran
down down the staircase
and over the wide sweeping stairs
and turned the gardens
red

Decks, movement, imagination creates this . . .

and
suddenly
everything belonged
to everyone again . . .

Suddenly . . . soldiers, women . . . alert . . . observe
the shoes . . . the house . . .

Theresa
God in Heaven!

Mary
Holy Mother!
It's true?

Marie-Therese
As true as I stand here.
Things as they are
people as they are
what else could happen?

I must go through all the bedrooms
get all the trinkets gold silver gems
coins notes

I need a dress with concealed pockets!

Theresa
I must go through the kitchen cupboards
get all the knives forks spoons the
spirits all the good wine

I need a big case with
a false bottom!

Mary
I must get up on the
roof . . .
strip all the lead guttering slates
gargoyles

I need a cart!

They pillage.
    Violent, Fabian, Obseno start taking shoes.

Lapin
    The papers!
    The files!
    Records! data! case histories!
    Get them!

    Conrad and Lapin start collecting papers.

Maria
    You collect your possessions
    camera passport money

    She does but . . .

    your visa your visa
    your papers which protect you!

    Hands shaking, she tries to find them . . .

Madame
    Car!
    Guards!
    Immediately!

Flavia
    No, Madame. No.

    She backs away, exits.
        Everyone suddenly focuses on Madame. Feste,
    Andreas approach her . . .

Feste
    Everything
    belongs to everyone!

Andreas
    Fuck!
    Yes!
    Fuck!

They seize her.

Maria
You have come from a country
where this doesn't happen
you switch on the light
light
you switch on the warmth
warmth
it is war.

Violent, Obseno, Fabian come towards her.

Maria
Do you show courage
understanding
female solidarity?
humanity?

*Feste and Andreas take Madame off somewhere to
rape her . . .*
    Andreas, Violent, Obseno drift towards Maria . . .

Maria
to men . . . very definite, very fierce . . .

Maria
Journalist!
British!
Protected!
Official!

Pregnant!

Mother!!!

*Violent, Obseno, Fabian back off . . . go to watch
Feste and Andreas . . .*

Maria
You don't know which works.

You're just thankful it does.
Something somehow saves your sweating
thank God! privileged skin!

And what happens
happens to someone else.

Madame (*off*)
Noooo!!!!

As . . . men observe, while . . .

Violent
Came on a terrorist once
four of us
cornered him in a lift
wasn't working
soon as we put a gun to his head
here
belly
here

Madame (*off*)
Please!!!!

Violent
pees himself
then
smell of shit
pathetic!
Shot him, the dog!

Obseno
Two of us
night
under a hedge
fucking platoon walks right into us!

Madame (*off*)
Oooooh!

Obseno
> We start giving it pow pow pow
> before they've time to realise . . .
> I mean, we total half
> rest fucking off like rabbits!
> Just luck
> but
> Shite!

Fabian
> Best Times, though!
> Fucking Adventure!

> *Madame, off, screams.*

> Danger's what you pay, right?

Violent
> Comradeship, though!

Obseno
> The Shags!

Fabian
> The Highs!

Violent
> Don't get that fucking peacetime!
> Gonna remember this our
> whole fucking lives!

> *They all cheer something off . . . rush to join . . .*

Conrad (*to Maria*)
> Cigarette?
> Ah . . . *pregnant!*

> *He lights a cigarette as . . .*

> They're peasants

> no education hardly . . .

no civilisation . . .
me education
me civilisation

and young

practically . . . *boys!*

and

times like these

shit happens

right?

He saunters off.
    Men run out, high as kites . . . one or two with items of Madame's . . .
    They dance off.
    Maria stands, picks up a shoe . . .

Maria
One shoe
looks like
a glass slipper.

She looks at it as Madame enters . . . horribly shocked, diminished . . .

Madame
Oh!

Everyone has gone!

It's not allowed!

My clothes are dirty!

Someone's disarranged them!

When The Generalissimo comes . . .
he will . . .

someone should put the lights on
it's very dark in here

Maria
and she looks
towards the darkest corner of
that terrible house

She looks towards the darkest corner of the house . . .

and sees
does she see?
is it real?

is it the light through the trees . . .?

an old man (*woman*)
in a leather apron
he's (*she's*) stitching

*There sits an old man in a leather apron . . . making
something. He talks to Madame . . .*

Shoemaker
what a lot of shoes
well made
expensive
lovely leather
lovely stitchwork
the craftsmanship!

are they all yours?

Madame
Yes.

Maria holds out the glass slipper . . . Madame takes it.

Shoemaker
Think of the work that's gone
into all that!

Eh?

Madame finds the other glass slipper.

Get much wear out of them?

Go far in them?

You know
a shoe's just something
to cover the human foot
for warmth
for comfort
no big deal
made from leather
which comes from
animal
which comes from
earth
which itself comes from a
great bang
at the beginning of time
so you see
we shoemakers know a
thing or two about
elementary construction!

More work making a shoe
than a baby!
Lot less fun!
Call me God!

Can I take a look at your shoes?

He/she takes her glass slippers.

Make 'em?
Buy 'em?
Earn 'em?

Don't suit you.
Not comfy.

Getting your bones all
out of whack!

He gets hold of her, quite gently.

What I'd say to you, little shoe
with my needle in your heart
my nails in your foot
my hammer tapping you on
your decorative skull is . . .
I think you need to
change your shoes . . .

Madame
Who are you?

Shoemaker smiles.

Where did you come from?

Smiles.

Go!
Go! Go! Go!

Smiles.

. . . please! . . .

Lapin!
Conrad!
Guards!
Women!

Women enter. Flavia has joined them.

Marie-Therese
It's true!

Theresa
It's not true!

Marie-Therese
It is!
ah!

Theresa
Oh!

Mary
So!

Marie-Therese
Just Madame!

Flavia
Just Madame!

Theresa
Wanting her clothes changed, I suppose!

Marie-Therese
Yes.

They ignore her. Try on shoes.

Anyway
he left her alone
in this beautiful room
in this great big house
in the very old green green woods!

Theresa
Oh!

Marie-Therese
You can never trust men like
that when they've done all their
tricks you can't see them for dust!

Mary
Aye!

Madame
Please . . .

Four
Shush shush shush . . .

Marie-Therese
and she went barking howling mad!

Three
Ouf!

Marie-Therese
She began to see people
in the corner of the room!

Theresa
God in Heaven!

Mary
Holy Mother!

Marie-Therese
She'd see
as if it were really there
an old man/woman in a leather apron
stitching a piece of leather!

Three
Ayee!

Madame
but that's . . .

Three
Yes, Madame there there there!

Marie-Therese
and she said that
this shoemaker got up
and spoke to her . . .

Theresa
What did it say?

Mary
Its voice

Marie-Therese
in a small clear
old man's voice

Theresa
Ouf!

Marie-Therese
it spoke
obscenity
unnatural ways
the magic arts!

Theresa
God in Heaven!

Mary
Holy Mother!

Marie-Therese
It told her to forget all
the things she felt were true
all the things she held dear
all she believed
she was not to believe
and in order that this
be carried out
the ghostly shoemaker
sat always in the room with her
and the poor mad girl
believed for ever after
that the ghostly shoemaker
was always with her!

Theresa
God in Heaven!

Mary
Holy Mother!
It's true?

Marie-Therese
As true as I stand here.
It happened in this very vicinity.
Everyone knows about it.
Everyone keeps quiet about it.
There!

They each have a very nice if highly unsuitable pair of shoes on. Madame walks forward and points to the Shoemaker.

Madame
Aaaayyyyyeeee!!

The Shoemaker smiles and puts a finger to his/her lips. Madame falls in a dead faint.

Marie-Therese
Fainted dead away.

Theresa
What's brought this on?

Mary
What's all this about?

Flavia
I looked after her like a Queen!

Marie-Therese
We looked after her like a Queen!

Mary
Never a foot wrong.

Marie-Therese
Holy Mother!

What day is it?

Theresa
When was the last time she
and the Generalissimo ...?

Mary
When did she last bleed?

Marie-Therese
should we make her pure again
for the Generalissimo?

Theresa
should we make her clean again
for the Generalissimo?

Mary
should we make her empty again
for the Generalissimo?

Theresa
that's our job
cleaning

Flavia
Yes.
Yes.
Yes!!!

They go to kill her as ...

All
death is small
it happens only once
how small it is ...

a rose fades
drops from its vase
onto the cloth

a fish jumps
clear of the stream
catches a fly

a bird dives
into the wood
claws in a mouse

a star dies
light years away
more darkness there

death is small
it happens only once
how small it is . . .

*They struggle and try to harm her physically. They
cannot . . .*

Marie-Therese
It's true.

Theresa
The shining truth.

Marie-Therese
Anyway
when it came to it
there in that rotten empty house
the women
with every motive for revenge
could not raise their hands
to kill . . .

Theresa
God in Heaven!

Mary
Holy Mother!
It's true?

Marie-Therese
As true as I'm standing here.
It happened to my grandmother.
It happened to my mother.
It happens to me.
I cannot do it!

Lapin enters with Conrad.

Lapin
Ah Good!
Destroy the evidence!
End the Thing!
Killed her already!!!

Marie-Therese
No we . . .

Theresa
Haven't as yet . . .

Mary
She's still . . .

Lapin
Breathing!
Kill her!
Kill her!
This . . . little . . . dolly here . . .
is the last very last piece
left of this old jigsaw!!
Break her into bits!
Do it!

Marie-Therese
It's true!

Theresa
It is!
The shining truth!

Marie-Therese
Last miserable piece.

Mary
But we can't!

Lapin
Women!!!!

Conrad! Be a Man for us!

Kill her!

Conrad
I can't!

I can't!

Some men can't!

Lapin
Men!!

Lapin seizes a knife, approaches Madame.
Madame wakes and stares at Lapin.

Madame
Holes, Lapin.
I keep thinking of holes.
I keep thinking I am holes
holes for people to put
. . . things in . . . their fingers . . .
their . . . excuse me . . . cocks . . .
put their babies in . . .
take them out . . .
put food in me . . .
wine . . . fine

wine . . . but . . . another hole!
and these . . . ears . . . the most open
of holes . . . no rest for them ever ever . . .
his words by day his gasps his grunts
by night by night his snores!

She looks at the three women and Maria.

And all the stories!
Oh the stories!
I am quite . . . pregnant with stories!

These are the worst holes of all,
Lapin!
What is the knife for, Lapin?

Lapin
It's for . . .
It's to . . . (*She can't do it.*)
Bureaucrats!!

Madame
Oh!
It's to . . . it's to kill me . . .
isn't it?
Oh, of course . . .
I'm sorry . . . I'm such a stupid . . .
another hole
yes
yes
go ahead.
Do it.

No one moves.

It's only fair.

No one moves

Please.

No one moves.

I don't think I love the
Generalissimo any more.

Madame breaks down.

Maria
You're visa'd passported tagged.
Files exist electronic computerised
numbered cross-referenced you.
From a country where you're
on file, numbered, docketed, credit-rated
rubber-stamped.
You can't be lost.

Someone comes forward as officials take her.

You're picked up
escorted
flown out
to your home
where
touch a switch
light
touch a switch
warmth

Travel sounds, jet . . .

and

Someone brings . . .

hot chocolate . . .

The smell pervades . . .
    *Madame starts to undress herself. Gets herself
ready for bed . . . T-shirt . . . trackie bottoms . . .
bedsocks . . .*

Marie-Therese
Anyway
she did what any broken-hearted
woman would do
she took to her bed

Madame gets into bed.

and for a while she lay
empty
tired
alone . . .

Madame lies curled up, then . . .

Madame
I need something to read.

*Three women start bringing her books . . . first one . . .
then pile upon pile as . . .*

Marie-Therese (*reading*)
This is a cracking story!
Dreadful goings on!
but . . . (*Looks to end of book.*)
the heroine survives!

*Lapin, with her knife, takes an apple, sits on the bed,
cuts a slice of apple, gives a piece of it to Madame*

Marie-Therese
She read
Jean Jacques Rousseau
Lamartine
Thoreau Saint-Just Auguste Blanqui
Barbes Raspail
and she read

*Lapin gets a book, gets into bed with Madame. They
both read. Three women bring books . . .*

Mazzini Marx Engels
Bakunin Alexander Kerensky . . .

Lapin
Any by women?

Marie-Therese
Alexandra Kollontai George Eliot
Mary Shelley Gloria Steinem
Susan Sontag Alice Walker
Zora Neale Thurston . . .

*The soldiers return to the periphery. They read books
too . . .*

Theresa (*reading*)
This is brilliant!
Tale of suffering
horror
but . . .

Sneaks look at the end.

human being
wins through!

Mary (*reading*)
. . . hey! . . . war!
this is about love love love . . .

Conrad (*reading*)
. . . this is about inventions
. . . travel . . .
discovery . . .

All tuck themselves up in bed . . .

Marie-Therese
and she read
and reading
she fell in love

with
a beautiful idea
a kind strong passionate idea
a gentle loving passionate idea
in the books were words as
wild and whirling as a kiss
ideologies as exciting as
an embrace . . .

Madame (*reading*)
Peace.

They all start reading from her book.

All (*reading*)
Peace.

Madame (*reading*)
. . . building . . .

They are hard to understand.

making . . .
creating . . .

Lapin
This is better than sex!

Conrad
This is nearly as good as sex!

Theresa
This is nowhere near as good as sex . . .
but . . . a varied life!

Marie-Therese
philosophies that fluttered
concepts that clung
emotions which pierced
her very heart!

Madame (*reading . . . complicated things*)
 revenge!
 creativity!
 accomplishment!
 love!
 pity!
 forgiveness!

Marie-Therese
 She read until the first
 grey light of dawn.

 Beautiful lights of dawn colour the stage . . .

Madame
 Hungry!

Lapin
 So thirsty!

 They all get the Generalissimo's feast. One by one, the soldiers return.

Madame
 Revenge.

 She hits one across his face. Then another, then a third, then . . .

 Pity.

 Forgiveness.

 She stops hitting. . . . gives Andreas a piece of bread.

Andreas
 The Generalissimo lay in a pool
 of blood.

Marie-Therese
 It's true!

Feste
Fuck!

Fabian
His brains plastered
the interior of his
not-quite-bulletproof car.

Theresa
This meat is . . . yumm!

Violent
Dead at the hand of one of his
not-quite-devoted
adjutants

Madame (*to soldiers*)
Hungry?
Thirsty?

Obseno
If they waited for him
they would wait for ever

Feste
Yes!
Fuck!
Yes!

Madame serves them food, drink . . .

Mary
Is there just a spot more of the . . . mmm!

Marie-Therese
They enjoyed what he would
have enjoyed
if he had not been
permanently delayed.

Lapin
This cheese is just ripe enough!

Conrad
Just!

Madame
They toasted him
as if he had just
become a proud father.

They lift up their glasses and drink . . .

Madame
to . . . Peace!

All
to Peace!

*Shoemaker comes forward with a pair of stout,
sensible shoes . . . holds them out to Madame.*

Shoemaker
I've made you some new shoes.

Maria
You leave Illyria.
File your story.
The horror. The devastation.
You blow up like a Michelin Woman.
You have a baby.
He's the most
beautiful
perfect
baby in the world!
Born into light warmth safety.
Toast.
Hot chocolate.
He's a month old.

It's January.
As Madame put on her new
sensible shoes
you put on yours.

With a pram . . .

You're on a walk.
You walking, Christmas coat,
pushing him, spanking new pram,
courtesy Grandma.
You leave the dog-walkers behind.
The joggers.
You're in a wood.
The sweet smell of rotting leaves.

One of the listeners gets up as . . .

Then
through the wood
this Man
his shoulders up
something . . . off about him
no shirt black pullover
he's not wearing a coat
walked past us
too close
not looking
never looks up . . .

in all your years of foreign reporting . . .
feeling the pop of a bullet beside your ear
here . . .
lying under a tree trunk in snow there . . .
looking up at the iron belly of a
gunship there . . .

nothing
compares to the terror you feel

thinking
someone is going to hurt your baby . . .

She stares at the man . . .

and

you look at him!

They stare at one another.

he knows you will kill

and he goes . . .

He sits down among the listeners.

You feel uncomfortable even
mentioning them in the same breath . . .

war
you
but until that wet day in the woods
you had not even begun
to understand the pain of war . . .

Madame
I have been idle

lazy
slow

I have been waiting for
the Generalissimo

and
he's not coming.

I think I'll get dressed now.

How do I look?

Music.
The Illyrians take up position.

Maria looks at them.
They look at her.
Music begins to build.

Maria
In that country
famous for
its war
its green green woods
its music
its dancing
that new morning
Madame looked ready.

Music swells.
All the Illyrians come forward and dance . . .
a good, strong, stamping, kicking, twirling dance . . .
Maria watches with her pram, pushing it
backwards and forwards in time with the music.
Lights fade.

The End.

MORE LIGHT

More Light was first performed in the Cottesloe
auditorium of the National Theatre, London, by
Sandbach School, Cheshire, as part of the Connections
season on 14 July 1997. The cast was as follows:

More Light Robert Cox
Love's Gift Chris Fitzsimmons
Many Treasures Lee Morris
Pure Heart Mike Lewis
Pure Mind David Critchley
Pure Joy Simon Hopkins
Scent of Ginger Nathan Hawley
Love Mouth Craig Bevan
Playful Kitten Paul Sloss
Little Friend David Robinson
Rapture Chris Williams
Moist Moss Jakub Burgis
Shy Smile Josh Jeffery
Fresh Morning Jonathan Williams
Sparkling Eyes Connal Shields
Perfect Pleasure Matthew Oram
Concubines Ben Cleaver, Kieran Johnson,
    Craig Sandlands
Man James Billington
Modern Men Dave Johnson, John Stawpert
Martial Artists Dominic Fernandez, Alex Greenwood,
    Chris Holmes, James Hutchin, Dave Johnson,
    John Stawpert

Design and Direction John Lonsdale
Lighting Designer Richard Howarth
Musical Director Kath Hudson
Choreography Maggie Gaston
Percussion Assistant Robert Martin
Sound Chris Thompson, Lynn Tomlinson, Mark Tudor
Lighting Assistants Chris Dowell, Mark Toshack
Stage Manager Chris Fitzsimmons
Costumes Norma Bayley, Sue Cleaver
Wigs Joan Owen
Jewellery Rosie Culling
Sculpture Callum Moncrieff
Origami Kelvin and Rebecca Stancombe
Voice Work Clifford Crewe
Martial Arts Dave Johnson
Props Karen Powell
Set Construction Tony Harrison
Production Assistants Jane Lonsdale, Lee Morris
Stage Crew Adam Bayley, Chris Cleaver

Characters

The Ladies of the Emperor
More Light
Love's Gift
Young Friend
Fresh Morning
Many Treasures
Rapture
Sparkling Eyes
Moist Moss
Playful Kitten
Scent-of-Ginger
Shy Smile
Love Mouth
Pure Heart
Pure Mind
Pure Joy
Perfect Pleasure

Man
a convict

Modem Man
Modern Woman

Act One

ONE
THE DARK AGES

There is darkness.
  *There is the sound of wooden chimes blowing in the
wind. A single, nearer sound, as of a tinderbox struck.*
  A small light appears.
  We smell sandalwood incense.
  *The light picks out the face of a young woman. She is
dressed in an enveloping black cloak, but we cannot see
this. All we see is a whitened face, eyes, a red mouth. She
speaks.*

Woman
  In the twentieth year of his rule
  the all-powerful Emperor
  now in sight of Death's gates
  gave thought to the construction of his tomb . . .
  To the high-ceilinged palace
  were admitted
  mathematicians astrologers metalsmiths
  artists architects inventors.
  Each put the most splendid workings
  of his mind upon paper
  and rolled out the paper
  so that covering the Emperor's tables
  was the most splendid Art
  of the most splendid minds
  in the Empire.
  And soon, in his all-powerful mind,
  the Emperor saw his tomb.

  A sound of galloping hoofs.

Leaving the palace at dawn
with only four soldiers
he mounted his horse and rode east.
At dusk,
having ridden all day, he stopped,
dismounted and said,
'Here is where my tomb shall be.'
And so it was
for the Empire was his
and the gentle hill on which he stood
was his
and the red sun which lit the hill
was his.
The four soldiers marked the place.

In the high-ceilinged palace
on his return
the all-powerful Emperor
summoned one of his Guard.
The Guard moved silently through
the sleeping palace.

She listens.
  Four screams fill the air.

As the sun rose
four soldiers in the palace did not.
The punishment for this infringement of
rules
is flogging.
This did not greatly trouble the four
soldiers,
now in Death's kingdom.

Some miles off from the gentle hill
a tunnel was started.

The tunnel,

dug day and night by the Emperor's
convicts,
approached the hill.

The Emperor,
his body now frail
but his all-powerful mind not,
entered the twenty-first year of his rule.
There were many celebrations.

Fireworks briefly illuminate the space.

The tunnel reached the hill.
It was wide and high.
The Emperor's convicts worked and slept
in the tunnel.
The smell of their bodies
was wide and high.

In the light of many lanterns
the hill was hollowed out.
Above, spring turned to summer
autumn to winter
day to night.

Beneath the hill
it was always day
for the work was continuous
and it was always night
for it was always dark.

The cavern
they hollowed out
was enormous.

Mathematicians   astrologers   metalsmiths
architects   inventors
rode on horses along the wide high tunnel
into the hill.

They dismounted
and with their Art
began to prepare the tomb.

The tomb was like this.
Such Art!
The ceiling was the night sky
above the Empire.
Artists painted it the deepest blue.
Their arms ached with the work.
Every star was in its place,
a jewel cut and set by the most precise
of jewellers.
The floor was the map of the Empire,
fields, woods, houses, roads, the skill of
gold- and silversmiths,
the three mighty rivers
made, in this tomb,
from quicksilver,
dry to the touch
and flowing from source to end
by the art of engineers.

Three gates there were to the tomb
set within three walls.
Mounted at each gate
was a pair of mechanical archers.
Anyone entering these gates
uninvited
into the tomb of the Emperor
would be shot with silver arrows.
Such Art!

In the centre
beyond the third gate
was the entire army of the Empire
cast in bronze

with which the Emperor
would fight his enemies
in the realms of Death.

In truth
the Emperor's tomb
was the most splendid
of all the wonders accomplished in his
rule.

The Emperor
now with one hand knocking at Death's door
said,
'So that my tomb
may be my final resting place
and so that my body
will not be disturbed,
let it be made clear
that all those who have worked on this
tomb
shall die with me.
They shall stay in the tomb,
the gates will be locked,
the entrance sealed
and no one on this earth
will know where my tomb is.
This Art will survive in perfection.
And I will be as inviolate in death
as I was in life.'

A bell starts tolling far away.

So it was
that at the outer wall
stood the Emperor's convicts,
at the middle wall
stood
architects   astrologers   metalsmiths

artists   architects   inventors,
the most special minds in the Empire.

The Emperor
now with both hands
pulled at Death's doors
and they parted.

'Take me to my tomb,'
he said.
And the ones so honoured to escort
the Emperor
on his last journey
were those of his ladies
who had borne him no son
and were to tend his body
within the inner gate.

The Emperor walked through Death's doors.
'More light,' he said,
and his ladies
held lanterns close to his body,
but he did not see,
for Death's doors had closed upon him.

And so it was,
walking beside a dead man,
my hands burning from the lantern,
I,
one of his ladies
who had borne him no sons,
entered the tomb.

Many lanterns provide more light.
   *The woman takes off her dark cloak. She is wearing
a magnificent eastern gown, lacquered wig, white
powder, high platforms supporting bound feet. Her
name is More Light.*

TWO
MORE LIGHT

More Light
    I have had a most wonderful life.
    I have known only the finest of food.
    I have slept on the softest sheets.
    I have known only the Emperor.
    My garden has been green.

    I walked the wide road to the tomb
    ready to serve my Emperor.

    Death is an honour
    in such company.

    The wide road came to an end.
    Our procession stood at the outer gate.
    It opened.

    She takes out a fan.

    Such heat.

    She opens her fan.

    Such a smell of unclean bodies.

    She uses her fan to waft the air. She is short of breath.

    I lower my eyes.

    She lowers her eyelids modestly. Her fan covers her
    face but not her eyes.

    Saw this way and this way
    shapes, men, eyes watching.
    The convicts I think.

    Her eyes dart and sidle.

We pass through the outer gate –
it closes.

She is more breathless.

Our procession at the middle gate.
More heat still.
Men stand
looking. I lower my eyes.
Put up my fan.
The most special minds of the Empire
mathematicians   astrologers   metalsmiths
artists   architects   inventors
eyes watching.
Men, I think.
So
the middle gate
opens,
closes.

Her eyes fix on something ahead. It is horrible.

Our procession
at an end
at an end
at the inner gate.

It opens,
it closes
for ever.

She looks towards us. Her eyes are blank and dark.

My garden has been green.
My face is white.
Inside my head it is black, it is black,
it is black.
I am twenty years old.

*Everything goes black. She screams and screams and
screams.*

THREE
BEFORE DEATH'S DOORS

Light returns suddenly.

A screen or curtain has been removed and sitting in a row, in the inner gate, are the Emperor's ladies who have borne him no sons. They are of all ages, from sixty down to six. They are all dressed as concubines, ladies of the court, wealthy whores . . . there are countless examples in the different periods of art to choose from.

They are all painted with white paint. More Light sits with them. They will sit quietly like this for as long as possible. When it becomes unbearable, More Light speaks.

More Light
  No one has spoken
  since the Emperor died.
  All of us women sit in silence,
  backs straight,

Some backs are straightened.

  hands still.

One pair of hands flutters and is still.

  What to do

Their faces express apathy.

  but sit and die
  with our Emperor?

They sit still for another long time.

  We are hungry.
  We are thirsty.
  What shall we do?
  We have known only the finest of food.

We have slept on the softest sheets.

Our garden has been green.
We have known only the Emperor

All eyes look modestly down.

and now his soul lives behind
Death's doors
and we sit before them,
our minds on his empty body.
What shall we do?

I look at them,
the Emperor's ladies
who have borne him no sons.

She names them. Each one makes a small, precise
acknowledgement of her name.

Love's Gift
Young Friend
Fresh Morning
Many Treasures
Rapture
Sparkling Eyes
Moist Moss
Playful Kitten
Scent-of-Ginger
Shy Smile
Love Mouth
Pure Heart
Pure Mind
Pure Joy
Perfect Pleasure

They all start to rock piteously.

Piteously they rock.
What shall we do?

FOUR
A BIRD IDEA

More Light
My mind washes.
I am in fresh air.

*Wind blows. It is cold and fresh. More Light takes a
sheet of paper. She proceeds to make an origami bird
as she reveals the image in her mind.*

I see an egg
in a nest
on a cliff above the sea,
although I have never in my short life seen
a sea.
I hear a 'chip chip'.
A small hole appears in the brown-speckled
shell.
A beak.
An ugly damp matty head appears.
An ugly damp matty bird falls from the
broken shell.
It dries in the sun.
It grooms itself.
It is sleek, it has feathers, it has wings.
It stretches and launches itself over the
cliff.
It drops.
It steadies itself on the air
and then it flies
up into the wind,
up into the sky.
The sun warms it.

The bird is now constructed.

I look at the ladies.
Piteously they wail . . .

The ladies wail.

Eat him I say.

FIVE
MORE BIRDS MAKE A FLOCK

The ladies all stop wailing at once.

More Light
Eat him I say.

The ladies' eyes go round. Their mouths open in an 'O'.

Each painted red mouth
in each white-painted face opens.
He is our Emperor.
He has always fed us.
He would not want us to go hungry.
Let us eat him.

Each lady takes a sheet of paper and constructs an origami bird. They are considering the proposition.

If we leave him too long
he will not be fresh

and we have known only the
finest of food.

More Light is playing with her paper bird.

The most special of dishes.

The finest cuts of meat.

We have always eaten royally.

I am so hungry.

What else is there to eat?

There is silence. The ladies finish their birds. They contemplate them.

There is silence.
All eyes look down modestly.
Then
one red mouth opens.

A lady's mouth opens.

Love's Gift . . . ?

Love's Gift
Sister, how shall it be done?

A great sound of birds' wings flapping. If only the paper birds could fly away in a great white flock, this would be wonderful.

SIX
THE ROYAL ARMY
PROTECTS AND SUCCOURS ITS LADIES

More Light puts an elegant finger to her chin to ponder the question. She walks a little. The ladies watch with rapt interest.

More Light
Ah!

Ladies
Aaaaaah!

More Light
Perhaps we can borrow some
utensils

from the Emperor's own bronze army
of death?

*Stirring, impressive, solemn martial music. The ladies
remove a screen, revealing the head of a phalanx of
bronze military figures.*

Each bronze warrior stands
his bronze weapon in his bronze grip.
The entire army of the Emperor,
each face individual,
each belt fastening,
each link of chain mail lovingly wrought.
Such Art!
I take a bronze sword.

She does.

Pure Heart takes a bronze dagger.

Pure Heart does.

Pure Mind takes a bronze axe.

Pure Mind does.

Pure Joy takes a bronze helmet.

Pure Joy does.
    *They return the screen. As they do, they hear the
sound of men's voices.*
    More Light continues in a whisper.

At the wall we hear
a voice, many voices.

Voices
    Who is that?
    What is happening?
    What is going on?
    Have you food?

304

The ladies freeze.

More Light (*still in a whisper, this time informative*)
 The mathematicians   astrologers
 metalsmiths   artists   architects   inventors
 the most special minds in the Empire.

The ladies are impressed.

We say nothing.
We, the Emperor's ladies,
speak to no man but
the Emperor.

All ladies are in full agreement here.

SEVEN
THE EMPEROR

*The ladies remove another screen and there, lying in
state on a bed, is the Emperor.*

More Light
 The Emperor lies asleep
 in Death's arms.
 The ladies of the Emperor
 remark on his deathly form.

Rapture
 How still he is!

More Light
 Rapture gazes.

Moist Moss
 How blue-white his skin.

More Light
 Moist Moss touches his cheek.

Shy Smile
How cold he is.

More Light
Shy Smile touches his hand.

Perfect Pleasure
How fat he is.

More Light
Perfect Pleasure lays both hands
upon his richly embroidered chest.

Perfect Pleasure
Sister . . . how is it to be done?

More Light
All eyes, all white faces, all round
red mouths turn to me.

They do.

Take off his clothes.

As they do, More Light contemplates.

We have undressed for our Emperor
many times.
He sat on cushions of silk
as we unwound our sashes,
opened our robes,
stepped down from our shoes,
rolled our white stockings down past
our knees, over our ankles, off our toes,
one by one
unpinned our hair
and combed it with our fingers
down over our marble breasts.
His eyes followed our every move.
Now we undress him.

Fresh Morning unfastens the row of
pearl buttons
on his embroidered coat.
She works from neckband to hem.
Her fabled fingers fly.
Moist Moss and Scent-of-Ginger shell the
Emperor of his coat.
He is very stiff.
Their celebrated strength succeeds.
Little Friend takes off his jewelled shoes,
his white socks off his toes,
one by one.
Pure Heart, Pure Mind, Pure Joy
ease off his silk trousers.
The Emperor lies naked
but for his golden war helmet.

*The ladies put up their fans to hide their faces. More
Light stares at the Emperor.*

I have never
looked at him like this.
He has always looked at me!

*She puts up her fan. The ladies simultaneously bring
theirs down.*

Ladies
I have had no joy of
the Emperor.
He lay on his bed.
I stood at the foot.
He stared at my face.
Two girls,
thirteen years old,
pour oil onto their hands,

Dance with their hands.

Anoint his loins.
Such Art.
Mould with the hands,
shape with the hands,
the soft, soft clay there
into something,
caressing, kneading, moving, shaping,
sculpturing,
turning soft clay,
firing soft clay,
into hard, firm, erect Male Figure Sculpture.
I crawl from the foot of the bed
on hands and knees,
Round Female Sculpture.
The two girls help me,
help the two sculpture figures,
become one.
I am hard dry clay.
Ah Ah Ah.
Art is Pain.
I feel a hand over my face,
the hand of the Emperor.
It turns my head,
turns the Female Sculpture
through ninety degrees.
Ah Ah Ah
Art again   Pain again.
I make no sound.
My face shows pleasure.

Many Treasures
Sister . . . we have taken off his clothes.

Playful Kitten
Apart from his golden helmet . . .

Rapture
  Dead
  as dead . . .

Love Mouth
  in his huge golden war helmet . . .

Sparkling Eyes
  naked as naked . . .

Playful Kitten
  with his small white love-member . . .

*They put up their fans. We hear a giggle. Fans start to
shake. One by one the fans come down and everyone
is grinning, then giggling, then chortling, then
laughing. They try to show respect for a while. They
fail. They fall about, hit each other, cry with laughter.
More Lights lowers her fan and watches.*

More Light
  This is what they fear,
  those who hold empires,
  that we will look and really see.
  The Emperor is dead.

EIGHT
SEVERING THE PAST

More Light
  I lift up the bronze sword.

*She does.
    The ladies fall back.*

The ladies melt back into the gloom.
I stand before my Emperor.
I use all my strength.

The sword goes 'clish' in the air
and I slice through his left shoulder
clear to the bone.

The ladies gasp and ululate.

A thick line appears in the skin,
the flesh parts.
My mouth is dry.

Rapture
Sister,
the limb is not cut through . . .
Perhaps if we bend back the arm
we might sever the tendons
as one might snap off a chicken wing . . .

More Light
Fresh Morning and Many Treasures
take the arm.
They twist it.
Then there is a sound worse than any
I have heard . . .

The ladies keen.

It is the shoulder socket dislocating.
I lift the sword again,
'clish' the blade arcs down,
and the Emperor's arm drops to the floor.

Moist Moss
Oh, sister . . . it is done.

She pats More Light's sword arm.

Many Treasures
Hard work . . . butchering.

Playful Kitten
What a lot of flesh on a man's arm . . .

She examines the shoulder.

Perfect Pleasure I am so hungry!

She kneels on the floor.

Love Mouth (*pouting*)
But . . . raw meat . . . my
stomach is too delicate for raw meat

Shy Smile
Look . . . the lanterns . . . they still
burn . . . perhaps . . . if we made a fire . . .
we might roast the Emperor's arm.

*A sound of a fire crackling. It roars. The area is
suffused with flame red. Then darkness.*

NINE
MANY TREASURES

Light up on Many Treasures.

Many Treasures
The Emperor's arm tastes
of venison.

*This is all very new and interesting. Many Treasures
is interested in the art of cooking.*

Slightly gamey with a suggestion of salt.
I think we roasted the arm too quickly . . .
the outside was scorched
and the meat nearest the bone too raw.

Our cooking improved.
The ladies of the Emperor are noted for
their quickness.
Their brains are not softened by
childbearing.

His legs tasted of roast pork!
His ribs of beef.
His feet of duck.
His innards made a fine stew,
thick, good gravy, with many tasty lumps.
His member was soft and tasted of cheese,
but we all knew that,
for many of us
had tasted it before.
The Emperor
with his fine strong body
shields us from death for many days.
The Emperor protects us
in death
as he did in life.

TEN
MORE LIGHT EXAMINES SCULPTURE

*Lights up on More Light, alone among the bronze army.
She is contemplating the figure of a soldier. She looks at
its forthright stance, its open face, and compares it with
herself.*

More Light
The inner gate is strewn with bones.
The air smells of cooked meat and
tallow grease.
The ladies' faces are no longer white.
The red paint is gone from the mouths.
The skin is dank, yellow and smutted.

Our bellies are round and full as if we bear sons.

*She strokes the face of the warrior. Then his chest,
then his legs, then his feet.*

Various ladies appear.

Love Mouth
Sister . . . the Emperor is almost gone.

She nibbles a fingerbone.

Smell-of-Ginger
Sister . . . the Emperor is almost used up.

She scrapes a piece of skin.

Pure Mind
Sister, the Emperor can no longer

Pure Heart
provide for us.

Pure Joy
What is to be done?

More Light thinks.
   The various ladies think.

More Light
Our brains are small,

This is demonstrable from the bronze warrior.

unused but for pleasure pastimes.
For help in this most difficult
problem we must look to the most special
workings of the most special minds in the Empire . . .

Love Mouth
The mathematicians

Scent-of-Ginger
astrologers

Pure Mind
metalsmiths

Pure Heart
   artists   architects

Pure Joy
   inventors

More Light
   who occupy the middle gate.

   All faces turn to the wall. They listen.

Love Mouth (*quietly*)
   We have heard voices,

Scent-of-Ginger
   the sounds of motion,

Pure Mind
   cries even,

Pure Heart
   but it is not our practice to talk with other men.

Pure Joy
   We ladies talk only to the Emperor!

   They tiptoe to the wall screen. They listen.
     All is silent.
     They all whisper.

Love Mouth
   Nothing.

Scent-of-Ginger
   Perhaps they are all asleep.

Pure Mind
   Perhaps they are all weak with hunger!

Pure Heart
   Perhaps they are all dead . . .

Pure Joy
For they have not had the protection of the Emperor!

They listen.

More Light
There is no sound beyond the wall.

More whispered conference.

Love Mouth
If they are all dead
we must collect them and cook them.

Scent-of-Ginger
Pickle them!

Love Mouth
Before they go off!

Scent-of-Ginger
Ay . . . what a waste of meat!

Pure Mind
We must find out the state of matters
beyond the middle wall!

Pure Heart
Sister.

They all turn to More Light.

Pure Joy
What is to be done?

More Light
We must prepare!

*The ladies watch as she starts to remove her
high-heeled shoes. She makes her clothes comfortable.*

The ladies understand. They remove restricting garments – corsets, restraining bodices, tight unbendable sleeves.

They borrow pieces as needed from the bronze army. They start to move, then almost dance, in a much freer, more open way.

They hear chinking and clanking. It is their jewellery – bangles, necklaces, earrings and rings. They remove them.

Pure Joy
How well we move!

Pure Heart
How free!

Pure Mind
How light!!

All Three
Sister, what is to be done?

More Light
We must open the door
and take a peep!

Ladies
Yes!

Pure Joy
Ayee . . . but the mechanical archers!
They will fire on us!

Ladies
Ayee!

More Light
No . . . no!
The mechanical archers
fire out
not in!

Love Mouth
They will fire upon the mathematicians

Scent-of-Ginger
astrologers

Pure Mind
metalsmiths   artists

Pure Heart
architects   inventors

Pure Joy
all the most special minds in the Empire . . .

More Light
who Built This Tomb!

ELEVEN
OPENING THE GATES OF KNOWLEDGE

More Light
Take hold of the left handle,
Pure Mind.

Pure Mind
Yes.

More Light
Take hold of the right,
Pure Heart.

Pure Heart
Yes.

Pure Joy
Now!

They open the gates. There is the sound of mighty doors opening in a vast building.

All the present ladies follow More Light through the gates.

Pure Joy remains with us. She is well-mannered and loves beauty, so she describes the gate screen to us.

The gates in the middle wall
are exquisite,
of beaten gold and silver.
They bear pictures of the triumphs
of the Emperor's rule.

A sound rends the air. Two arrows travelling at speed. Then silence.

Pure Joy gasps with fear and clutches her heart. She listens. Nothing. She continues to entertain us.

Of beaten gold and silver,
they bear pictures of the triumphs
of the Emperor's rule.

She loves detail.

Here is his army victorious in battle,
here are his road-builders reaching the
farthest outposts of the Empire,
here are his tax collectors in a small
village collecting corn,
here is a thief, having his hand cut off,
here are his stonemasons building a
great wall in the north.
Around the gate handles
choirs sing praises
and hosts pray.

There is a knocking at the gate.

Who is it?

From behind the gates.

More Light
 Open the gates, fool!

*Pure Joy abases herself for us at More Light's rudeness
as she opens the gates.*
 *Another sound of two arrows travelling at speed.
The sound of muffled screams from behind the gates.*
 *The party of ladies appears, dragging or carrying
two men sitting bound and cross-legged, their mouths
oddly full and each with staring eyes and arrows
embedded in their hearts.*

 Shut the gates, fool!

*More abasement from Pure Joy for More Light's
rudeness as she shuts the gates.*

Scent-of-Ginger
 My heart pounds!

Love Mouth
 My mouth! Dry!

Pure Mind
 My palms! Moist!

Pure Heart
 I have wet myself!

Pure Joy abases herself.

Ladies
 Oh oh oh oh oh!!

They scream.

More Light
 Quiet, fools!
 My head is full with your wailing.
 I need to think!

They are silent at her fierceness.

She kneels down before one of the corpses.

This was Clever Hands
the inventor.
He it was who made the water flow
upwards to the higher fields.
He it was who made the device which
turned the ox carcass so that it
roasted evenly.
He it was who made the mechanical
singing linnet for the Emperor's
third son.
He it was who made the mechanical
archer which has now shot him
through the heart.

Love Mouth
Sister . . . we are all hungry . . .

Scent-of-Ginger
Sister . . . we must attend to him
before he goes off . . .

More Light
Who bound his arms and legs?

She feels in his mouth, takes out rags.

Who gagged him?

Love Mouth (*to Pure Joy*)
Make sure the gates are secure.

Scent-of-Ginger
The important thing is to eat!

*Pure Mind, Pure Heart, Love Mouth and Scent-of-
Ginger take the bodies away to the other ladies.*

See what we have found!

Many Treasures
  Ayee!

Love Mouth
  An inventor!

Playful Kitten
  This is Sees Future, the astrologer!

Many Treasures
  Thinner than the Emperor
  leaner flesh
  tougher
  more consistent of texture . . .
  Careful braising, I think . . .

They take the corpses behind a screen. There are the shadows of swords raised, the sound of dismembering.

TWELVE
THE MIDDLE GATE

Pure Joy
  It is written
  in works of astrology
  that the astrologer can foretell
  everyone's future
  but his own.

More Light
  Beyond the gates there
  we peered into the blackness.
  All is silent.
  But no . . . we hear breathing.

Love Mouth lifts the lantern.

Everywhere

eyes
low
staring up at us,
row upon row of eyes
staring out from the most special minds
of the Empire.
Their feet and hands
are bound.
Their mouths stuffed with rags.
Two move not at all.
Arrows in their hearts.
'Take these two,'
I hear a voice say.
The ladies look at me.
It is my voice.
They move along the seated trussed men,
the most special minds of the Empire
and drag away the two carcasses
across the floor
and through the gate
to eat.
What of our future?

Pure Joy
    Sister, we are in a tomb.

THIRTEEN
A MEAL

Many Treasures brings on a steaming cauldron. The ladies coo and flutter with pleasure. They line up, each with a bronze helmet. Many Treasures ladles steaming stew into each one.

Love's Gift
    I have a little more than my sister.

Fresh Morning
Ah no. I am happy.

Rapture
Little Friend is still growing . . .
Perhaps another spoonful?

Sparkling Eyes
How carefully cut is the meat!

Many Treasures
The size of a walnut.
The best size.

Rapture
Little Friend . . . Playful Kitten . . .
take the soft place.

Scent-of-Ginger
Heaven in the mouth!

Many Treasures
Not too melting?

Ladies
No, no. Not too melting at all!

Pure Joy and More Light enter.

Many Treasures
Casserole, dear sisters?

Pure Joy
Aaah!

*Playful Kitten gives her helmet of stew to More Light,
then goes and lays her head in Rapture's lap. Playful
Kitten is very young.*

More Light
This is yours, Playful Kitten.

Rapture
You must eat, little sister.

Many Treasures
Perhaps cut up the pieces to
pistachio size, sister?

Playful Kitten
It makes me dream.

Rapture
What does it make you dream, little one?

Playful Kitten
Bad things.

Rapture
What bad things, little one?

Playful Kitten
I become a big bad thing
and I roar
and I stand in the dark
and my chin is hair
and my eyes look at me
and want to watch me all
the while
and I hurt between my legs.

She puts her face to Rapture's lap.
The ladies have stopped eating.

Rapture
I have this dream too, little sister.

She strokes her head.

Love Mouth
I too.

The other ladies nod.

Love Mouth addresses Many Treasures.

It is no criticism of your cooking!

Ladies
No! Oh no, no!

Love Mouth
We are simply doing wrong.

Ladies
Yes! Oh yes!

More Light (*laughs*)
Yes!
We are the ladies of the Emperor!
We are here on this earth to serve
the Emperor . . .
to please him
to amuse him
to bear him sons!
But we have not borne him sons . . .
So we must serve him in other ways!
How?
Let us go with him through Death's doors!
Yes!
Let us walk with him!
But wait!
Where is he?
Where is he, Playful Kitten?

Playful Kitten
We ate him, More Light.

More Light
We ate him!
He was good to us, Playful Kitten . . .
better than he knew!
For he is now in us!

He occupies our bellies
as if he had given us sons!
We have his dreams!
Ladies, we are now all . . . all . . .
Emperor of all we survey!

The ladies ponder this.

Pure Joy
It is written
in studies of other religions
of a religion whose devotees
eat of the body of their god
and drink of his blood
and their god lives in them.

More Light
I am Emperor here.
I believe this is possible.
Playful Kitten, do you believe
this also?
Little Goddess.
Child Emperor.

More Light abases herself before Playful Kitten.

Playful Kitten
Yes!
(*Imperiously.*) Hand me my helmet!

Many Treasures (*equally imperiously*)
More casserole!

The ladies resume eating.

Pure Joy (*thoughtfully contemplating her casserole*)
If it is true that we are all now
the Emperor
for he is now one with us

326

All ladies nod.

by the same token we must all be

She takes a mouthful . . .

inventors

She takes another mouthful.

astrologers
for they too
are now one with us.

More Light
What of our future, sister?

Pure Joy
Let us have one, sister!
Let us be Emperors of our world.
Let us be its
mathematicians   astrologers   metalsmiths
artists   inventors
architects.
As the Emperor constructed his tomb
so let us construct our world!

*The ladies dress Playful Kitten in the dead Emperor's
clothes.*

Playful Kitten
It's a game?

Pure Joy
It's a game!

Playful Kitten
I'm an Emperor!

FOURTEEN
THE EARLY RENAISSANCE

More Light
In the first year of her rule
the all-powerful Emperor
now in sight of Death's gates
gave thought to the construction of her
world . . .
to the high-ceilinged tomb
were admitted
mathematicians astrologers metalsmiths
artists inventors architects.
Each put the most splendid workings
of her mind upon paper
and rolled out the paper
so that covering the Emperor's tables
was the most splendid Art
of the most splendid minds
in the Empire.
And soon, in her all-powerful mind,
the Emperor saw her world.

*The ladies, who have adopted new attitudes as the
Emperors and the most splendid minds in the Empire,
contemplate their world.*

FIFTEEN
THE EMPEROR LEAVES HIS PALACE

Pure Joy
Such Art, sister.

More Light
What else have we?

328

Many Treasures
Sister . . . a word.
The inventor is on his last legs . . .
Someone must go beyond the gate.

More Light
Why me?

Many Treasures
The ladies are occupied.
Constructing . . . inventing . . .

Pure Joy
You are our Empire's sword.
Without this our world is threatened.

More Light
I have had a most wonderful life.
I have known only the finest of food.
I have slept on the softest of sheets.
I have known only the Emperor.
My garden has been green.

Pure Joy
I will open the gate.

More Light
My voice is no longer low and melodious.
It is harsh as a sword stroke.

> *More Light takes a sword.*
> *The gates are opened by Pure Joy.*
> *We hear the sound of two arrows through the air.*
> *More Light walks into blackness.*

I can see nothing!
Fool!
I search with my hand out in front
of me for dead men.

A sharp intake of breath.

I smell a wide, high smell!
There is something here.

We hear women's voices ululating.

I light my lamp.

*She lights her lamp. Light reveals her standing with
her back to us. Projected is the shadow of a huge
man.*

Aaagh!

The man's arm rises. It holds an axe.
    More Light turns round.

Aaagh!
Standing before me,
an axe in his hand,
is a man.
The axe is raised.
It is made of bone!

The light comes up to reveal exactly that.
    Furious drumming. Women wailing.
    Then darkness.

Act Two

ONE
PURE JOY OF ART

A sound of something musical, between a xylophone and a celeste. The notes are tentative, exploratory.
The lights reveal Scent-of-Ginger among the bronze army. She tries out notes on various bits of the bronze soldiers.

Scent-of-Ginger
Tsk!
Ah!
Bah!
They are so out of tune!

She takes out a percussion instrument composed of hung helmets, daggers, belt buckles etc. She plays a melody on them.

Hmm.
Yes.
I see . . .
It all needs rearranging!

Nearer, lights reveal some of the ladies posing. Above them is a mobile of origami birds.
Love Mouth is sketching them.

Pure Joy
Love Mouth draws us all for a
composite group portrait.

Love Mouth
Don't move.

Pure Joy

    None of us is moving.
    Trained only for politeness,
    respect and servitude,
    we struggle like crawling toddlers
    towards the skills of creation.

Love Mouth

    Daaghhh!

Pure Joy

    I find myself the stillest of us
    all for I am thinking.
    What Art?
    Hundreds of years hence
    people will penetrate this tomb
    and they will see the painted sky
    studded with jewelled stars,
    the rivers of quicksilver,
    the mechanical archers,
    the gates,
    the bronze army,
    and say,
    'Look, it is the sky,
    the stars, the rivers, archers,
    the gates, and that must be
    the army!
    What Art!
    And look, in this middle section here,
    these skeletons, wrapped in fine clothes,
    these must be the women!
    What were they doing here?'

Love Mouth

    Keep still!

Pure Joy

    And one of them, keener-eyed than

the rest, may find, among the dust,
the shape of a bird,
and he will touch it
and the old old paper bird will
fall to dust,
and he will say,
'No, I was mistaken,
it is nothing,'
and will turn back to the beautiful
gold and silver gate.

Love Mouth
Hold your heads a little more.

They all hold their heads a little more . . .

Yes, that's pretty, yes.

Pure Joy
So I keep still,
while my eyes and mind scamper and
scrape like a rat about this monument,
looking,
looking for the post and lintel
on which to rest the architecture
of my dis-ease,
for the arch to take the weight
of my fear,
for the rib vaults and flying buttresses
to hurl my hope stone-like
into the ether.

Love Mouth
If you want to be part of my
picture, sister . . .
you must Keep Still!

Pure Joy keeps still.
Love Mouth sketches.

I am going to put us all
in the palace garden.
With the sun coming through the trees.
Flowers in the grass in the foreground.
A table with food.
Dew-dropped fruit.
Red wine in a glass flagon.
In the background the village
of my childhood just under
the mountains.
An early evening sky.
And we will all be smiling
in delight!

Phhh!
Well . . . rest a while.

Love Mouth contemplates her work furiously.
Pure Joy rises.

Pure Joy
There are no flowers here.
No sun.
But I remember.
Do I make flowers?
We are in a tomb?
Do I show Death?
We are in a hell.
Do I create hell?
We construct a world.
Do I show hope?
What colour is hope?

Playful Kitten and Little Friend run on. They have
tied long ribbons to the end of bronze daggers. They
play with them, slashing the air with random trickles
and blazes of colour. They run off.
   Pure Joy starts moving in time with the melody of

Many Treasures. She adopts a strong pose.

You remember that statue in the
Great Hall?

She slightly alters her pose.

The beautiful young man?
Walking forward.
Into the future.
The Kouros.
Feet planted firmly on the earth.
Strong limbs.
Striding forward.
Head high and proud!

All the women adopt the strong pose.

We thought him splendid!

Love Mouth
Oh, that is new! I need *more light*!

The lights fade.

TWO
ADAM AND EVE

*Lights up on the second gate. More Light, bound and
gagged, is hurled in by a Man, wild and hairy, who
sports a recent sword gash. He carries an axe of bone
and a bronze sword.*

Man
Can't run much, Royal Shag!
Can't run at all now!
Can't screech now, Palace Parrot!
Nice piece o' work this!

Indicates sword.

Nice piece o' work this!

Indicates sword gash.

Do it ta you now, eh?
Bleed blue, willya?
Cut off a wing, eh?
Taste of parrot, willya?
I've ett of the smart boys thought up this cage.
Tasted of paper and books.
Gotta taste for bird.
Eaten raw fowl before.
How I got penned in this hutch
For that big misdemeanour,
stealing food.
Mebbe make a big fire,
have
Sunday roast.
Right royal feast you'd be
Parrot.
Na . . . gonna take the stuffing outta
your crop, Polly . . .
an' ya gonna say who's a Pretty
Boy then to me
an' no screeching or your blue
parrot tongue's Pretty Boy's
first bite, am I clear?
Nod your head if you're a
talking bird!

More Light nods her head.
  He takes out the gag.
  She chokes and gags.

Too much dry corn, Poll.

He gives her water to drink from his hip flagon.

'Ave some pure fresh rainwater.
Courtesy the lads on the outer
gate.
Comes through the walls.
Very tasty tomb with running water
we got.
'Spect you're sipping purified silver
in the middle there?
Let's you and me talk, Parrot.
Emperor dead yet?

More Light
Yes. Man yessss!

He smites the air.

And maggots forever bite and chew
his fat carcass!
Yessss!
Fat bastard took along a flock
of you parrots.
Wass happened to them?

More Light
Dead. Every one.

Man
Every one but you, Poll.
How comes you still fluttering?

More Light
Same way as you, convict.

Man
You ett bird?

More Light
I ate bird.

Man
Yessss!
What it taste like?
Sweet?
Soft?
Chicken?

More Light
Sweet.
Soft.
Chicken.
Yes.

Man
Like that, me.
Like a taste of that.

More Light
But you can't taste that, convict.
It is all gone.

Man
Part from this, Poll.

He touches her.

More Light
Apart from this, convict.
Emperor's Parrot.
Whose voice sung him melodies.
Whose tongue caressed his ear.
Only the best for the Emperor.
Finest, softest of voices
talking to him only of pleasure
in his ear,
lips murmuring on his ear
of pleasure.

Man
Emperor's woman. Say what you did.

He puts his ear to her mouth.

More Light (*in a whisper*)
I gave him pleasure.
Only the best for the Emperor.
The most practised of touches.
The most elegant of movements.
The deepest of knowledge in how
to show the Emperor love.

Man
Show me, woman.
I'm Emperor here now.

More Light
Unbind me then, my lord.

Man What am I, a fool?

More Light
Yes.

Man
You're dead.

More Light
You also, fool.

Man
Then I'll go like an Emperor.
Die of pleasure from a
bird of paradise pecking
and feathers.

He unties her.

Show me the art of love,
Parrot.
I'm the Emperor.

More Light

He lies in his bed.
I stand at the foot.
He looks into my face.
I lower my eyes modestly
behind my fan.
Two girls,
thirteen years old,
pour oil onto their hands,

She performs all this for him.

anoint his body,

She begins to stroke him.

take away all his cares,

*She places the bronze sword and bone axe carefully,
usefully for her. He watches.*

anoint his head, his neck,
his shoulders stiff from battle,

She puts her hand inside his shirt.

his manly chest.
He has no breasts.
Anoints his thighs, his loins.
Such Art.
Mould with the hands,
shape with the hands,
the soft, soft clay there
into something
caressing, kneading, moving, shaping,
sculpturing,
turning soft clay,
firing soft clay,
into hard, firm, erect Male Figure Sculpture.
I crawl from the foot of the bed

on hands and knees,
Round Female Sculpture.

She begins to open his trousers.

Ah Ah Ah.
Art is Pain.
I feel a hand over my face.

The man takes her chin and directs her down to his lap. She looks at his lap.

Aaaaaagh!

Man
Squawking, Parrot?
Seen nothing like it, Parrot?
Different diet, Poll?
How will you eat this chopped-about delicacy?
What Art is needed here!

More Light
Who did this to you?

Man (*takes hold of her*)
Who did this to you?

THREE
RIBBONS OF COLOUR

A lantern appears in the darkness. Lightens to reveal Playful Kitten and Young Friend carrying their ribboned sticks.

Playful Kitten
Down here.

Young Friend
It's dark.

Playful Kitten
I'm the one who holds the light.

They would both prefer to be the one who holds the light.

That's the river.
It's poisonous but you can drink it
if you like.

Young Friend
No!

Playful Kitten
Drink it!

Young Friend
No! I drink blood!

This makes them laugh. Then scares them. They both would prefer to hold the lantern.

Playful Kitten
No!
I'm the one who holds the light!
We lie down here.

They lie down on their backs.

It happens when the lantern warms them.
It takes a while.

Young Friend
All right.

Playful Kitten (*pointing left*)
There's where it's darkest.
That's where Paa lives.

Young Friend
Oh. Who's Paa?

Playful Kitten
My friend.
He's an animal really but he can talk.
I won't let him hurt you.

Young Friend
What does he eat?

Playful Kitten
Dark.
He eats dark.
He chews it up and swallows it
and then he belches
and it makes light.

They giggle.

And then he farts
and it makes light.

They giggle some more.

And when he shits
he shits candles
and they're lit!

This is very funny.

And once he was sick
and it was a lantern!

This is even funnier.

You can kiss me.

Young Friend
All right.

She does.

Playful Kitten You can touch me if you like.

Young Friend
No, I don't want to.

Playful Kitten

All right.
You can hold my hand if you like.

Young Friend
All right.

They hold hands.

I don't like being touched.

Playful Kitten
I don't either really.
Not like that.
It's horrible really.

Young Friend
It's horrible.
Sister.

Playful Kitten
Sister.
Here they come.

Stars appear.

They're jewels really.
But they look like stars.

Young Friend
I once found a star.

Playful Kitten
Where?

Young Friend
In the grass. It was green and sparkly.

Playful Kitten
Did you keep it?

Young Friend
Yes.
But a robber stole it when I
was asleep.

They both play with their ribbons, swirling them in the air.

There's someone in the dark.
It's probably Paa.

Playful Kitten
Probably.

She is not so sure.

Young Friend
He might have woken up and be
hungry.

Playful Kitten
Yes.

Young Friend
He might belch some light.

A voice whispers from the dark: 'Playful Kitten . . . Young Friend . . .'

Playful Kitten
Help . . .

Voice (*whispers*)
Are you there?

Young Friend
Yes, Paa . . .

Voice (*whispers*)
Come over here.
Bring the lantern.

They go into the darkness with the lantern. It lights the face of Rapture.

Rapture (*hugging them and smacking them*)
Foolish! Foolish!
We thought we'd lost you!
Our sister is still behind the gates!
We are lost!
Bring the lantern!
How much light do you think we have!

She hurries them away.

FOUR
PERSPECTIVE

Rapture arrives with Playful Kitten and Young Friend among the ladies.

Rapture
Here they are!
In the dark!
These two at least are here!

Scent-of-Ginger
Foolish girls!
Did you hear anything?
Did you see anyone?

Playful Kitten *and* **Young Friend**
No.
Nothing.
No one.

Playful Kitten
Just the dark.

Sparkling Eyes
Oh, misery!

She bursts into tears.

Love Mouth
More Light has not returned!
What has happened to her?
Oh, it is all awful!

Many Treasures
We are so low on . . . ingredients!
What is to be done?

Pure Joy
A fine world!

Many Treasures
You were with her at the gates!
What happened, sister?

Pure Joy
She walked through the gates.
I closed them.

Silence.

I heard a scream.

Silence.

I came back to pose for Love Mouth.

There is nothing we can do!
There is nothing we can do!

Love's Gift
We could go after her . . .

Pure Joy
Why? Why? Why?

Shy Smile
To save her, sister . . .

Many Treasures
  And there is the matter of
  eating.

Love's Gift
  We should go after her . . .

Pure Heart
  It would be only fair . . .

Pure Mind
  It would be only polite.

Scent-of-Ginger
  It would be dangerous . . .

Pure Joy
  Dangerous?
  Polite?
  Fair?
  We are in a tomb!
  It is not the Emperor's any more!
  It is ours!
  We are dead already!
  This is the world of Death!

Love Mouth
  No! No! No!
  I am painting!
  We are all . . . making!
  For the first time in my life . . .
  it is . . . my life!
  I am . . . creating!
  Not Death!
  No!
  No!

Many Treasures
  And we eat, sister.

We eat.
We are alive still.
We are alive!

Pure Joy
We are eating human flesh!
What will we *not* do?

Many Treasures
Nothing.
There is nothing we will not do now!
Nothing!

(*To others.*) . . . Now, let us think
sensibly . . . What is to be done?

Shy Smile
It seems to me . . . excuse me . . .
there are three tasks to be accomplished.

Many Treasures
Yes?

Shy Smile
There is the getting of food.

Ladies
Yes.

Shy Smile
And the getting of our sister.

Ladies
Yes.

Shy Smile
And the getting on as normal.

Love Mouth
Yes. Creating.

Pure Joy
    As normal! Hahaha!
    As normal!

Love's Gift
    Some of us should see about the
    getting of food and the getting
    of our sister.

Shy Smile
    The two tasks . . .
    may be . . . may be one.

Ladies
    Ayeeee!

    They contemplate this.

Many Treasures
    So be it. Who will go?

    Show of hands.

    Who will stay?

    Show of hands.

    So be it.

    They look to Pure Joy. She has not raised her hand.

Pure Joy
    Love Mouth paints.
    Many Treasures cooks.
    Makes music.
    Playful Kitten dances.
    I have made nothing yet.
    Let me make a gesture.

    She takes a bronze dagger and puts it to her heart.

    Let me make a sacrifice.
    Here I am. Meat.

Many Treasures
 Sister, you have been meat long enough.
 Be a woman with us.

Pure Joy
 There is nothing worse than this!

Many Treasures
 Let us find out.

Pure Joy
 I'm frightened!

 She drops the dagger.

Many Treasures
 You're hungry!

FIVE
FAUVISM

The middle gate. More Light and the Man.
 They sit facing each other. Between them lie the sword and the axe. They are playing scissors, paper, stone. She is scissors, he is scissors. He has never played before.

Man
 More Light?

More Light
 Yes.

Man
 More Light?

 She is scissors, he is stone. He blunts her.

More Light
 I was named for my quality.
 The Emperor felt

when I entered a room
it became brighter.

He is paper, she is scissors. She cuts him.

Man
And you played his games?

More Light
He liked competitions.

Man
Emperor's favourite?

More Light
At first.
But I read, listened.
My mind grew.
More light in it.
He turned to softer, more
flattering flames.

He is stone, she is paper. She wraps him.

Man
You were sad?

More Light
I was glad.
My love for him was all Art.

She is paper, he is stone. She wraps him.

Man
Art don't work on me. Practical me.

More Light
Three. I win.

Man
Then choose, More Light.

She takes the sword.
    She is stone, he is scissors. She blunts him.
    She is scissors, he is paper. She cuts him.
    She is paper, he is stone. She wraps him.

More Light
    Three.

Man
    Choose, More Light.

She puts the sword to his throat.

Your death.
I choose your death.

Man
    Got hungry.
    Stole.
    Got caught.
    Got me balls chopped off.
    Dug a tomb.
    Got banged up in it.
    Whore stuck a sword in me gizzard.
    Did I live well!
    One last request.

More Light
    Of course.
    It would be only polite.

Man
    Make me happy.

More Light
    I can do nothing
    I say.

Man
    You can do this

He takes her hand, puts it to his cheek.

More Light
He says
and touches me so

He puts his hand to her cheek.

and so

She puts her other hand to his face

and so.

He puts his hand to her face.
They look at each other.

I can do nothing for you
I say.

Man
You can do this,

He caresses her.

More Light
he says,
and I touch him so
and so and so.

She strokes his face, his hair.

Man
Hurts . . . happiness,

More Light
he says.

Man
Worst pain . . . happiness,

More Light
he says.

Man
Makes ya think of the life
ya wasted,

More Light
he says.

She kisses him.

Man You using Art?

More Light
I don't know.

Man
Doesn't matter.

More Light
It does
I say.

*He kisses her. From the darkness come Scent-of-Ginger,
Pure Mind and Pure Heart. They leap upon him.*

Ladies
Excuse us . . . so sorry!

They hurl him to the ground.

Scent-of-Ginger
Forgive us . . . we must hold you down!

They bind him fast.

Pure Mind *and* **Pure Heart**
A thousand pardons . . . we must bind you tight!

Scent-of-Ginger
Gag him! Excuse us . . . you must make no sound!!

Pure Heart
What have you caught here, sister . . .
a philosopher?

355

More Light
Yes. A philosopher. Yes.

Pure Mind
Our sisters guard the gates!
We are hungry!
Hurry!

They hurry the convict and More Light through the gates.

SIX
SCULPTURE

Love Mouth among the bronze army. She is alight with excitement.

Love Mouth
I see it all now!
The light had to be in my head!
We must observe what has gone before!
How things were done!
We must see how the light in the
heads of our past masters struck
their space!
Of course!
By chipping and painting our friends
here . . . I destroy.
I take them into my head . . . transform
them with the light there . . .
the magnificent
correct
and knowledgeable play of
objects in light!
Yes?
Yes!

Yes! yes! yes!
I need something to make with!

The ambush party enters.

Scent-of-Ginger
Here . . . here!
If we bind him to this warrior he
will be held fast!

They bind him.

Pure Mind *and* **Pure Heart**
Excuse us . . . so sorry . . . just a little
tighter. There!

Scent-of-Ginger
More Light has lit our world again!

Pure Heart
Scent-of-Ginger will make such music over this!

They hurry off.

Love Mouth
More Light . . .
I have got all the other ladies'
likenesses in rough working form . . .
Would you be so kind . . . so gracious
as to spare me a short time for a
sitting?

More Light
I am to be painted? Again?

Love Mouth
Sculptured!
Three-dimensional!
Beautiful object!

More Light
Of what material,
Love Mouth?

Love Mouth
Of clay!

She hurries her off.

SEVEN
PAA

The convict is chained to the bronze warrior. He hears a noise. A whispering.
Playful Kitten and Young Friend appear.

Playful Kitten
Greetings, Paa.

Young Friend
Greetings, Paa.

Playful Kitten
We have to touch him, or he can
escape.

Young Friend
All right.
You first.

Playful Kitten
All right.

She goes to touch him. Runs back.

It's not frightening at all.

It is.

Now you.

358

Young Friend
All right.

She goes to touch him. Runs back.

Now he can't get us.

Playful Kitten
No.
Never.
He's dead.

Young Friend
Good.

Playful Kitten
I'm hungry!

She runs out.

Young Friend
Bad Paa.
Don't . . .

She goes to stand right before him.

Don't ever do that again!

She smacks him.

Ever ever again!

She smacks him again and runs off.

EIGHT
A FEAST AT THE HOUSE OF LEVI

The ladies sit, thinking.

Many Treasures
It is our world.

Ladies
It is. Yes.

Many Treasures
No one but us can say what is right
and what is wrong.

Ladies
No. No, they cannot.

Many Treasures
Therefore the decision is ours alone.

Scent-of-Ginger
We are all Emperors here!

Ladies
Yes. Yes we are all Emperors
here.

Many Treasures
So.

They think.

Shy Smile
It is but a short step

Love's Gift
But a very short step . . .

Shy Smile
From eating the dead . . .
to. . . making someone dead . . .
in order to eat them.

Ladies
Yes. Yes, a very short step.

Many Treasures
And we are hungry.

Ladies
We are. Indeed we are.
Starving.

Pure Joy
I have never been so hungry
in all my life.
I am sick with it.

Ladies
Yes. Yes, indeed.
We are all sick with it.

Playful Kitten runs in.

Playful Kitten
I am hungry.

Rapture
Shush now. Shush.

Young Friend runs in.

Young Friend
We should have a party!

Rapture
Shush now. Shush.

Pure Joy
We should have a party.
Celebrate this . . . Empire
we find ourselves in!

Ladies
We should. Yes.

Shy Smile
What else have we on?

Ladies
Exactly!

Many Treasures
We are back to the problem of . . .
provisions.

Rapture
We have just the one . . .
source.

Shy Smile
Which requires . . .

Ladies
attention.

Many Treasures
Sisters, what is to be done?

More Light and Love Mouth enter.

Pure Joy
Sister, is your sword sharp?

Many Treasures
We are preparing for a party!

Shy Smile
Sister, the guest you brought back
needs attention.

Love's Gift
He must be prepared for the feast.

Ladies
Our most important guest!

Many Treasures
Here.

She hands More Light the sword.

Prepare him, Sister.

More Light
Why me?

Scent-of-Ginger
    When we came to help you, sister,
    you were in great danger
    for your lips touched his
    and you were not bound.
    A test.
    We need this so.

More Light takes the sword and goes to leave. Pure Joy catches her.

Pure Joy
    Sister . . . if I may . . . I would be
    pleased to perform this task
    for you . . .

More Light
    He has been cut about all
    his life!
    He is a man
    but he is not a man!

Pure Joy
    No one but you or I shall
    know of this.
    Give me the sword.
    The deed is done.

More Light
    How will you do this deed,
    Pure Joy?

Pure Joy
    I will take the sword so . . .
    Find his heart so . . .
    and with all my strength . . .
    push.

More Light
  You will leave him bound?
  Leave in his gag?
  Tied to a piece of the Emperor's Art?

Pure Joy
  I am a lady of the Emperor, Sister!
  I cannot fence with him until he
  drops!

More Light
  Why do you want to do this deed,
  Pure Joy?

Pure Joy
  I have done nothing.
  Ever.
  I am without Art!

More Light
  Pure Joy.
  You give pleasure.
  You are justly named.
  It is enough.

Pure Joy
  It has no heirs.
  It leaves no fortune.
  It does not survive.

More Light
  You remember Laughter . . .
  who died in childbirth . . .
  at the palace . . .

Pure Joy
  Yes.

More Light
  Her jokes?

Pure Joy
Yes.

More Light
When she dressed up as the Emperor?

Pure Joy
Yes.

More Light
Your face lights up.
Your heart warms.
She is dead.
It is enough.
Give me the sword.

NINE
THE IMPRESSIONIST

*More Light goes to the bronze army. She takes the gag
out of the convict's mouth. He spits in her face. She nods.*

Man
Bitch.

More Light nods.

Bastard.

More Light
That, too.
Shall I cover your eyes?

Man
No, bitch.
I want to watch you at your work.

More Light
So be it.

She lays the sword at his breast.

Any last requests?

Man
Listen to my song, Parrot.
We're digging out,
us lads.
We dug in . . . we can dig out.
Got the clever boys telling us where
to dig . . . using their most special minds to
fashion tools for us.
We're going to get out, Cage Bird,
What do you say to that?

More Light
You're sure?

Man
I'm sure.
We're men.
We got brawn, we got brain.
Be out in the open very soon.
Going to be free.
Breathing fresh air.
Not this meat-filthy soup.
What do you say to that?

More Light
Not you though.

Man
Less you let me go.
Less you and me slip away in the
dark like thieves in the night.
Take you with me.
Outside.
Fresh air.
Free.

Empire.
Gentle hill.
Red sun.
What do you say?

More Light
I say.

She plunges the sword into him.

Die!

Man
Aaaaaagh!
Bitch!
Fool!
Bitch!
Why?

More Light
It would be no different!
For the Empire was his
and the gentle hill on which he stood
was his
and the red sun which lit the hill
was his!

He slumps.
  She holds him.

It is too late for us.
There would be no change.

Man
You daft bitch.
You'll never know.
Kiss me.

She does. He dies. She cradles him
  The ladies come and take him away. More Light cries
pitifully.

TEN
AN OBJECT PLACED IN ITS ENVIRONMENT

Love Mouth enters carrying something covered in cloth.
Playful Kitten and Young Friend carry lanterns.

Love Mouth
Sister?
Sister . . .
I have something to show you.
Put the lantern . . . there.
And that one . . . here.
And this . . . THE OBJECT . . . here.
I
More Light . . . look what I have made!

She takes off the cloth. It is a paper sculpture . . .
quite small . . . of the ladies of the emperor.

See . . . it is us!
A bit rough . . . an early piece . . . but . . .
here is Playful Kitten . . .
and Young Friend . . .

Playful Kitten
We're dancing!

Love Mouth
Here is Many Treasures . . .
stirring a pot of . . .
Here's Rapture . . . Love's Gift . . .
Fresh Morning . . . Sparkling Eyes . . .
Scent-of-Ginger . . . Pure Joy, Pure Heart,
Pure Mind arms about each other . . .
Perfect Pleasure . . .
Me . . . hands making . . .
and look . . . look . . . who is this
holding up a lantern?

More Light
  More Light?

Love Mouth
  More Light.

Young Friend
  I'm dancing!

More Light
  So you are.

Love Mouth
  I place it here,
  close to the bronze army
  but not of it, do you see?
  When, many years hence,
  people of the future gaze on this place
  they will say,
  'Aaah,
  Aaah . . . this is to do with this
  and this is to do with this.
  How very interesting Art is!'

ELEVEN
A FESTIVAL OF ARTS

Music plays. Playful Kitten and Young Friend run off.
  A procession of the ladies enters, some playing.
Playful Kitten and Young Friend are dancing. Other
ladies bring on a steaming pot that smells of cooked
meat.
  They take up the exact position of the small sculpture.

Love Mouth
  You see!
  You see?

Exactly as we are!
But for me with my hands in clay
and you, More Light,
holding the lantern!

Many Treasures
Sisters . . . our feast.

Ladies
We are hungry.
We are starving.
We are ravenous!

Scent-of-Ginger
How good it smells!

Young Friend
I'm so hungry!

Love Mouth
I have deserved this!
All this . . . creativity!

Pure Heart
Have my seat, Sister.

Pure Mind
No, no, take mine!

Pure Joy
My headache has quite gone!

Shy Smile
I am getting quite used to this
darkness.
I see quite clearly!

Ladies
Yes, yes!
The eyes get used to it.
One adjusts.

Rapture
  And one adjusts to the amount
  of air.
  It is quite fresh.

Ladies
  Yes, yes!
  It feels quite fresh!
  It feels like fresh air!

  More Light looks up.

Shy Smile
  One adjusts.
  How miraculous the human body!

  More Light stands.

More Light
  It is lighter.

Ladies
  One adjusts.

More Light
  It is cooler.

Ladies
  It feels like fresh air.

More Light
  It is fresh air.
  Listen!

  Silence. Then a sound of digging.

TWELVE
THE TRANSFIGURATION

The ladies all become quite still.

The light grows and grows from a central source high above. For the first time, natural daylight floods the tomb. A modern rope ladder drops into the centre of the space.

A Man, dressed in modern dress, descends. He looks around.

Modern Man (*soundlessly*)
Christ!

A Woman in modern dress comes down the ladder. She stands with the Man. They look around.

Don't touch anything.

The Woman looks at him wordlessly. He goes to the bronze army.

Christ!

She kneels to look at the paper sculpture.

Modern Woman
What's this?

Modern Man
Don't touch anything.

Modern Woman
This is falling to pieces . . . We must be . . .

The Man finds the women of the court.

Modern Man
Christ! Look at these!

The Woman goes to the ladies of the court.

Don't touch anything!

Modern Woman
Poor bastards!

She reaches out gently to touch the face of More Light, as the Man calls up the ladder.

Modern Man
Get down here and have a look at this lot!

There is a sound of rustling and movement of old layers of dust. From the ceiling flutter and drop millions and millions of origami birds. The Modern Man and Woman watch them silently as the lights fade.
  Music.